Designing & Building
YOUR CUSTOM DREAM HOME

How to Create an
Experience You'll Love to Remember

PAUL MUELLER, SR. & PAUL MUELLER, JR.
with Suzanne Ratti

ISBN: 978-0-578-66320-3

Edited, designed, and published by: Ideas360llc.com

www.MuellerHomes.com

TABLE OF CONTENTS

Introduction

For as long as I can remember, I've had a passion for building things. It seems our entire family has always enjoyed designing and building things. My great grandfather was a woodworker and custom cabinet maker. My father was a professional engineer who founded a successful engineering business. He instilled in me a strong work ethic, a desire to chase perfection, and a valuable business acumen.

In 1992, after more than ten years of working in a variety of roles within the trade and construction industries, and serving as a leader for a large nationally-known production company, I started my own construction business – Mueller Homes. Despite my experience, I realized I had a lot to learn. But, they say experience is the best classroom, and little by little, I learned how to not only build a quality home but also how to run a construction business. My family's core values and strong work ethic served me well and allowed me to create a company that is still recognized across the industry for our pursuit of excellence.

From the Author

Paul Mueller, Sr.
Founder, Mueller Homes

As the business has evolved, we have survived the highs and lows of the real estate and construction industries. This is not by coincidence, but rather through careful planning and sensible business decisions. Unfortunately, we have also seen our fair share of colleagues and competitors succumb to tough times. Through it all, however, we have always maintained the highest integrity and quality standards and I believe this is the foundation that has allowed us to succeed.

Why We Wrote This Book

Over the years, we have been honored to work with hundreds of clients to create a one-of-a-kind custom home building experience. We believe that the *experience* should be memorable – one that is fondly reflected on for many years, as you live, work, entertain, raise a family, and even retire in your home. So, our primary goal in writing this book is to educate and inform you on the critical elements that we have found essential to creating that memorable, one-of-a-kind experience.

We have seen the great, the good, the bad, and the ugly side of the construction industry. And, unfortunately, there are far too many horror stories of what can go wrong with the custom home building process. We have actually 'rescued' several families in these situations. These stories are not meant to create fear but to convey the importance of making informed decisions and to help you avoid being one of those stories.

We believe it's important for you to understand the entire process and key factors before you select a builder and begin building a custom home so, we provide many examples in this book to illustrate these concepts. These concepts may be obvious to some, but for most people, we hope this book can provide you insight that can save you considerable time, money, resources, and yes, even tears.

Analogies Worth Considering

We have struggled for years to help clients understand the unique complexities of custom home building and the importance of having a wonderful experience, in the process. After all, it is one of the few times where you make a choice to trust someone else with a decision that will truly last a lifetime. It is very tough to come up with analogies that capture this thought and truly reflect the investment, the emotional experience, and the desired outcome. While we still aren't convinced these are the

<u>best</u> analogies, we want to offer these to you for consideration:

1. If you are considering marriage, the selection of your partner is not typically a quick process. After all, there are emotional, financial, and other long-term considerations. After you take that famous walk down the aisle, you will live with your decision for many years to come. In an era where the divorce rate is ever-climbing, parting ways can be emotionally and financially devastating. So, most people enter this decision-making process slowly and after careful consideration, knowing that this will be one of the most important decisions of their lifetime. Not to minimize the institute of marriage, but we feel that building a home should merit a similar process.

2. If you are contemplating elective or cosmetic surgery, you want the best! After all, your decision will be one that you will live with for many years to come. You will likely seek a referral from a trusted source, since you'll be making a considerable investment, but price is typically not the determining factor. You are likely more interested in finding a surgeon that is highly regarded, has tons of experience, and demonstrated results. You want someone that can provide what you seek, with minimal risks, and a track record of producing the desired results that you will live with for a lifetime. We feel that choosing your builder should involve a similar strategy.

We offer these analogies because to some, the custom home building process 'just comes down to price,' or perhaps a mindset of 'anybody can do it.' While the same can be said of many doctors, you would never go under the knife with someone you don't know and trust. Similarly, entering a marriage without knowing your partner and considering the long-term implications, would be careless.

So, our final piece of opening advice is to select your builder the way you would select a marriage partner or surgeon. Give careful consideration to the immediate and long-term implications of your decision. You will find this important thread throughout this book.

One Final Thought

We believe that an educated consumer will make the best decision. Our goal is that, armed with the information and knowledge provided, this book will allow you to make wise decisions and truly create the home of your dreams with an experience that you fondly reflect on for years to come.

We sincerely wish you a truly memorable custom home building experience.

Part 1

THE START OF A
BEAUTIFUL RELATIONSHIP

Chapter 1:

What Type of Builder Do You Need?

Before you begin looking for a lot, choosing a design, or selecting an architect or builder, it is important to understand some basic terms and concepts. This will help ensure your expectations and budget are met, in the most effective and efficient way possible.

Types of Construction/Builders:

- **Production** – A production home builder provides a large volume of housing to serve the masses. These types of homes typically include houses, townhomes, condominiums, etc. Production builders build the same homes over and over again with 'stock' plans and very little, if any, customization. These homes are generally the most affordable because the builder can buy land, supplies, and materials in bulk and move buyers through a very structured regimented process. A production builder is focused on the assembly line process and quality is generally adequate.

- **Semi-Custom** – A semi-custom home builder typically utilizes several standard home designs but may provide the home buyer with some flexibility and options for selections. An architect is typically not involved in semi-custom home building, and the home buyer's design and selection variables may be limited. This is a more affordable option for many homeowners who are seeking a more unique home than production, but at a lower cost and quality than custom home building. Most semi-custom builders do not have the capabilities, processes, or expertise to execute above-average levels of quality, but the homes they build can often be quite beautiful and more economical than a custom builder.

- **Custom** – Over the years, the term "custom home" has been over-used to describe a wide variety of home building styles, quality, and features. This spectrum and variation of definitions include production builders that have 'custom' departments, smaller builders who are actually operating a semi-custom model, and the truly custom home builder. Keep in mind that building a "truly custom home" requires a different process and approach. It is not simply a matter of incorporating custom materials or finishes – it requires a more complete skillset, comprehensive oversight, and processes. However, many production and semi-custom home builders have found that the term 'custom' can warrant significant price increases – so buyer beware! A genuine 'custom' home builder is one who has the processes and expertise to execute every design, element, and detail to meet the clients' exact needs. Every aspect of the building process is unique and the design, selection, and execution are critical to the end result and experience.

- **Luxury/Handcrafted/Fine** – These terms are used interchangeably to describe a high level of quality and customization, refined process, and a superior execution level that one expects from a one-of-a-kind luxury builder. These builders typically possess the experience, well-defined processes, and staff necessary to execute the highest level of quality, materials, and craftsmanship. These builders typically work collaboratively with the architect to create a masterpiece the client will treasure.

UNDERSTANDING THE SPECTRUM OF CUSTOM HOME BUILDING

Almost every builder seems to offer a 'Custom' Building' option, but are they really custom? The biggest challenge with customization is that it requires a builder to incorporate an entirely different skill set, process, and level of craftsmanship into their existing process.

Production Builder

With a "Custom Building" Department offers very little true customization and may find it challenging to successfully implement client customizations into their repetitious processes.

Price = $ Quality = ★   Customization Capabilities = 1

Semi-Custom Builder

Offering some variation in floor plans, finishes, etc. The semi-custom builder's business and construction processes are not designed for customization. Oversight and care of true customizations may require extra time on the schedule, additional trades and craftsmanship and may cost substantially more to accommodate client requests, or they may limit changes altogether.

Price = $$ Quality = ★★   Customization Capabilities = 2

Custom Builder

Adept at working with an architect to customize every aspect, architectural element, selection, and finish to your specific needs. The building process, schedule, traces and job oversight are geared towards implementing custom home design and modifications for increased efficiency and quality.

Price = $$$ Quality = ★★★★   Customization Capabilities = 3-4

Luxury Custom Builder

Provides a superior level of quality, construction, details and service throughout every aspect of the design, construction and finishing stages. Adept at working with complicated details, architectural elements, high-end materials and finishes. Processes, scheduling and oversight are designed to incorporate all of the necessary elements to deliver a on-of-a-kind home and client experience.

Price = $$$$ Quality = ★★★★★   Customization Capabilities = 5+

When selecting a builder, the type of construction, quality and customization capabilities are important. While price is obviously a factor, it is the selection of your builder, their overall building process, and the finished product that either creates a wonderful experience or a horror story. So, let's review how to select your builder.

Authors Comments:

Beware of 'custom home builders' that do not operate a truly custom home builder business model. They may charge more for 'custom selections or finishes' but their ability to provide you with higher quality, refined processes, and an enjoyable custom home experience may be a far cry from your expectations.

Chapter 2:

Selecting a Builder - A Long-Term Relationship

Building a custom luxury home is an accomplishment that, for many families, represents a certain lifestyle, level of status, and achievement. For many, it is a once in a lifetime experience and perhaps one of the largest single investments you may make. So, deciding who you are making this investment with is a big one!

We believe the builder selection process should be given the same careful consideration as any other long-term relationship. Once your choice is made, it's going to take a lot of hard work, good communication, and flexibility to create and maintain that relationship. Unfortunately, a relationship gone bad may create ill-will, may be challenging to terminate, and can cost a lot more than expected. If the relationship is built upon a solid foundation with a clear set of goals and mutual respect for one another, the chances for success are greatly increased and the overall experience can be extremely rewarding.

While no project is perfect, the reputation and integrity of your builder speak volumes. We've included a *Checklist of Questions to Ask A Potential Builder (Appendix Checklist #1)* that you'll want to use in helping make your selection. Most importantly, as we will discuss in the upcoming chapters, you'll want to answer some basic questions before moving forward with any builder:

1. Do I **like** the builder?

2. Is the builder someone I will enjoy working with?

3. Does the builder have experience with the type of home I'd like to build?

4. What do past clients and on-line reviews have to say about the builder/building experience?

5. What kind of processes does the builder have to ensure the construction stays on-time and on-budget?

6. Is your builder a good **businessperson**, as well as a good builder? Are his vendors paid on-time? Has he seen his business through up and down markets?

While the price is important too, we will explore price in much greater detail, later in this book. But, setting the price issue aside, there are a number of other factors that are equally important to your selection of a builder:

-   **Expertise/Expectations** – The industry is full of contractors and builders who are able to build a home. Unfortunately, it's also full of companies who may not possess the business acumen or construction knowledge to successfully execute the construction project. Each builder you interview should have expertise that they can bring to the overall experience. You should carefully consider your overall expectations before making a decision. Will the builder's experience and expertise allow them to provide a product and experience that will meet your expectations?

-   **Processes:** Does the builder have the processes in place to provide you with the type of home and experience you desire:

    o   What processes do they have in place to maintain on-time and on-budget parameters?

    o   Are they attentive to details?

- o Are they consciously focused on the carpentry and fine design skills you expect?

- o Will they approach the construction of your home as a custom-designed masterpiece approach or more of a commodity or an assembly line?

- o Are they sensitive to fabrication, installation, delivery of one-of-a-kind materials?

- **Handcrafted Materials, Fixtures, and Finishes:** Custom homes generally incorporate a variety of handcrafted materials not commonly used in a production or semi-custom home (i.e. high-end appliances, hand-milled wood products, finishes to match client selections, handcrafted wood cabinetry, geometric inlays, one-of-a-kind pieces, etc.) Just like cars, using high-quality selections and materials can create substantial cost differences and variables in budgeting. These materials not only meet a higher standard but often require more sensitivity when designing and installing. Does your builder have experience with these materials?

- **Staffing/Skillset/Band-with:** The capabilities and business model of the builder will heavily influence the type of client experience you receive.

- o Do they have the human, equipment, and capital resources to manage multiple projects?

- o Do they provide extensive oversight for project management?

- o Do they employ Master Carpenter vs. Jr. Carpenter or do they have any carpenters on staff?

- o Client Concierge – do they provide concierge services, someone working side-by-side with the client throughout each phase of the project to enhance selections, stay on schedule, and coordinate meetings and showroom visits?

- o Woodshop – do they have in-house fabrication or out-source?

- o Do they have in-house or sub-contracted workers and how long have these relationships been established? Are their sub-contractors reliable?

- **Permitting and Site Preparation:** A qualified builder will be well-versed in the permitting requirements for the jurisdiction you are looking to build. Areas like waterfront properties, forest preservation areas, and areas designated for controlled growth require in-depth knowledge and can be associated with considerable fees or lengthy processes. These should be discussed at the outset of the process to ensure your builder has the knowledge and expertise to guide you on this journey.

- **Collaborative Approach:** For luxury custom homes in particular, are they adept at working collaboratively with multiple professionals such as the Architect, Interior Designer, and Landscape Architect to ensure that your vision is carried out?

At the end of the day, the home building experience and the entire customer experience is largely based on the builder's capabilities in these areas. Be thorough in your evaluation. There are far too many stories of homeowners who 'wished' they had more thoroughly evaluated their builder or made a decision on _these_ factors, rather than price alone.

This long-term relationship between you and your builder will begin with the design and estimation, which can take many months to finalize. Construction can be from six to twenty-four months, or longer depending on the scope and type of home being built. After the keys are handed over, there will likely be additional information exchanged between you and the builder for many years to come with regards to warranties, vendors, and subcontractors. So, make your builder selection with a focus on the long-term relationship and you'll have a chance for a much better overall experience.

Authors Comments:

At Mueller Homes, we pride ourselves on our core values of integrity, trustworthiness, and honesty. When you talk with our clients, you will hear stories about how we treat our customers, the unique building experience we provide, and the way we work quickly to resolve issues as they arise. No one wants a stressful building experience. That's why, we believe, the selection of your builder is one of your most important decisions.

Chapter 3:

5 Important Considerations When Selecting A Builder

As we discussed in the previous chapter, selecting the right builder is extremely important. There are far too many stories where the decision to go with one builder over another was based on the <u>wrong</u> factors, and the building experience was less than desirable. We have actually 'rescued' a number of families from these situations. These stories are not meant to create fear, but to convey the importance of selecting the right builder for you.

When selecting your builder, we believe there are five main areas for consideration. We suggest rating each of these five areas from 1-10, for each builder you are considering, in order to help you select the right builder for you.

1. Experience & Longevity

When you are considering building a custom home, we cannot devote enough time or words to the importance of the builder's experience and longevity in business and in the construction industry. The home building industry, much like the real estate market, has seen it's fair share of ups and downs. In 2008 alone, it is estimated that nearly half of the home builders or contractors in business in Maryland **went out of business**. Unfortunately, many of these builders went out of business with the bank or their clients' money.

The number of years your builder has been in business is a testament in and of itself. It shows that they have weathered a variety of market conditions and understand how to start, run, and maintain a business. Experience also provides the best classroom for typical building challenges. An experienced builder will learn something from every home built. That kind of experience is immeasurable.

Technical skills are required to oversee handcrafted construction processes, materials, and methods, specifically for complex and luxury homes. Timelines and schedules will quickly fall behind if the builder is not adept at coordinating long-lead-time special orders, incorporating special one-of-a-kind pieces, and incorporating these considerations into the overall timeline. Not every builder has these skills and resources or understands the complexities involved in scheduling a custom home build.

Since the market is cyclical, there are a variety of vendor, supplier, and trade issues that impact the home building industry. A builder with longevity has typically established reliable partnerships that can withstand market fluctuations. In addition, they will likely be up to speed on local, national, and global supply issues that may impact the pricing or availability of certain materials. These issues can also impact whether or not your home can be built on the schedule required and for the budget allocated.

In conjunction with *Questions to Ask a Potential Builder (Appendix Checklist #1)* you'll want consider your builder's experience by discussing:

a. **Experience Running A Business?** – Some folks have technical building skills, but not a lot of experience running a business. It's important to ask: How long has the builder been in business? How do they manage cash flow? Do they maintain job accounts for each project? Are they current with their vendors and suppliers?

b. **Experience In The Industry?** – Some builders have a good understanding of how to run a business but do not possess the experience or technical know-how and vice-versa. This can often manifest itself in projects that are not executed effectively. The quality of a home's construction can be impacted by these deficiencies. Projects may also be over-budget, delayed, and eventually have significant cost-overruns. Either way, an experienced builder will possess both the technical know-how as well as the business insight to successfully complete a custom home project.

The experience and longevity of the builder are also good indicators of their business know-how.

2. The B-Myth (Business Acumen)

The business acumen of your builder directly correlates to your overall home building experience. Why? Perhaps you've heard of Michael Gerber, a best-selling author who wrote the world-renowned book entitled *The e-Myth*. The book is a must-read for entrepreneurs or start-ups because it describes, in detail, the three essential components a business needs to survive and the mistakes and pitfalls that must be avoided for every successful growing business. In the construction industry, it's very common for builders to enter the construction industry with common misconceptions about what it takes to actually <u>run</u> the business. We refer to builders without a strong business acumen as the *B-Myth*.

The *B-myth* is a relatively easy business model to spot. Typically, a carpenter or foreman decides to start up their own building or construction company with no skills or knowledge about <u>how to actually run a successful business</u>. Everybody's got to start somewhere right? But, perhaps you'd prefer they learn on someone else's home?

There are many clues as to a builder that is operating under the *B-Myth*. They likely have no administrative or support personnel, taking care of the necessary paperwork required to run a successful business. They may not possess the critical ability to manage cash flow, accounts payables, and long-term business planning strategies.

The consequences of this lack of experience can have a big impact on your project. They may be behind in their Accounts Payables to vendors, suppliers, and sub-contractors. They may not understand the importance or have the capability, to segregate funds by project. This is an important detail that can lead to many other problems because homeowner's funds are co-mingled and one project's surplus is helping to sustain the next one. They may only have enough cash flow for one project at a time, which can cause delays with the resources needed to run two or more simultaneous projects. This can create a domino scenario where supplies are late, sub-contractors aren't showing up, and suppliers won't ship products because they are owed money.

The builder operating under the *B-Myth* is a very risky situation for the prospective homeowner. Unfortunately, we have witnessed first-hand the consequences when this model fails. In one such case, the builder did not have the business experience and processes to properly maintain the business. So, while the home was under construction, the builder went out of business. The home was half-way built, with significant draws already made on the construction loan, and insufficient funds to complete the home.

This is not to say that start-ups don't have the capabilities to build a luxury home, but as a homeowner, you will want to carefully evaluate the level of business acumen your builder possesses to ensure that your investment is secure.

It is also important to note that a **builder's** business model is very different than a **remodeler's** business model. All of the processes and financial aspects of a custom home build are vastly different than a remodeling project approach. We strongly suggest that you only consider builders who have a strong business acumen for the entire custom home building approach.

3. Value Factors

Most of us appreciate a good value. Value typically involves considering a variety of factors - typically quality, price, service, and speed. For example, if we want the highest "quality" we are accustomed to paying more for it. Conversely, if we want the lowest "price" we expect to probably receive a lower quality. The auto industry always provides a great comparison for this discussion. Obviously, a Mercedes is priced differently than a Ford. If you purchase a Ford you aren't expecting a Mercedes level of quality and vice versa. Likewise, if you choose the lowest-priced builder, you will no doubt get what you pay for and you must be realistic in understanding that there are sure to be differences in the level of value or quality provided.

Each customer views value differently. Thus, we believe it's important to understand the difference between the four 'value factors' as it relates to the builder in each of these areas:

- **Detail & Quality** – A good builder will provide the desired detail and quality – in alignment with the price you are spending. The builder will encourage prospects to tour other homes, previously built, and review the standards of quality. They will be able to demonstrate ways in which they incorporate quality into their business. For example, we use dust covers on all of our projects to ensure that construction dust and debris do not contaminate the duct system. This 'extra step' is not standard by any means, but it's one of the ways we show our clients our extreme attention to detail and the high level of quality and detail we provide.

- **Service** – The key to great service is great communication before, during, and after the construction of the home is completed. How does the builder ensure this? Do they have staff, resources, technology, and processes that focus on maintaining a high level of service and communication? Do you require a high level of attention to your needs or are you willing to sit back and just wait for the final product?

- **Speed** – In most cases, you will have a construction/permanent loan, in which the terms are higher during construction and then convert after the home is completed. In this case, time equals money. You'll want a builder who has processes in place to create efficiencies and ensure the home stays on time. It is not uncommon for the schedule to slide in a busy market or when foul weather impacts the construction schedule. But, most reputable builders leave room for these variables and are able to accommodate accordingly.

- **Price** – If you are willing to sacrifice one of the factors above for a better price, then, by all means, do so. But, when determining value, remember that rarely is the lowest priced builder the best value. If they are lower-priced, they are often making sacrifices in one area or another and it is incumbent upon you to understand where those sacrifices are being made and if you can live with the end result.

The bottom line is that, as you select your builder, you'll want to be sure that you identify your priorities for each of these four areas. You may be willing to sacrifice service for price or speed for quality, etc. Likewise, some builders will excel in all areas while other builders excel in one area and not another. Some builders will provide a low price while sacrificing service or quality. So, when choosing your builder, it's important to factor 'value' into the overall relationship and pricing structure.

Ask yourself, "What do **I** value?" What are the most important aspects of the custom home building process for you and your family? For example, if the quality is important to you, you will expect to pay a higher price, but if the price is important, perhaps you're willing to sacrifice quality? If you want a home built quickly, maybe you will be willing to sacrifice a little craftsmanship to meet your deadline? If the cost of the project is most important, then perhaps you're willing to work with a builder that does not provide a high level of personal service and/or the highest quality. The value factors basically boil down to the age-old concept that "you will get exactly what you pay for." No amount of negotiating can override the costs and services needed to build a home, so be sure you consider the value you expect and ensure your builder is aligned with those concepts.

4. Cost/Price

As it relates to the builder selection process, we believe price should be <u>one</u> of the factors you consider, but certainly <u>not the most important</u> factor. In home building, if you are **truly** comparing apples to apples, one builder's price is not typically more than 5-8% from another. If the variable is more than that, you should be asking questions because there is almost certainly a discrepancy between the specifications, quality, or service level. Because there can be many variables to price, making it difficult to compare apples to apples, we have dedicated Chapter 4 to the discussion of *"Why Cost Can Be An Elusive Selection Tool."* Be certain to understand pricing and all of its complexities before making your builder selection.

5. 3 R's: References, Reviews & Resources

A builder should be able to give you multiple recent **references** and even some older references. If they don't want to provide more than 1-2 references, because they don't want you to 'bother' their clients, beware! Most happy clients are willing to share a few minutes of their experience but you should also respect the builder and their clients by only asking for, and contacting, references as part of the final phase of selection. Don't ask a builder for references until you have narrowed things down to the final 1-2 builders. Make sure you use the *Questions to Ask Builder References (Appendix Checklist #2)* included in this book.

Online **reviews** are also an important tool to use in your selection process. When considering reviews, you are looking for consistent feedback. Today's technology provides an opportunity for anyone who has had a bad day or minor disagreement to instantly share their opinions. So, weigh bad reviews with discernment.

Other **resources** are also available to assist you in your builder research. Google your builder and see what comes up! One of our clients googled a builder they were interviewing, and the most recent search revealed the builder had recently been featured on a news program for a scam. Check to ensure their state licensing is current and if they are part of any local builder's associations. Search local and state records by business or principal's name, search for liens or other contract disputes. Verify that they have current workers compensation insurance, and that liability insurance coverage limits are appropriate for the home you're building. You can also check with your local Better Business Bureau. While no business is expected to have a perfectly clean slate, you can again determine any consistent patterns, if there have been disputes, and how those disputes were resolved.

Authors Comments:

Don't rush to judgement if you see or read a bad review. There can be difficult customers in any business. The important thing is to use discernment to determine if there are <u>consistent</u> patterns of quality, service, or dissatisfaction. It may help to do some research, prior to calling references. Then, you can ask the reference about any specific issues that may have come up in your research, or if the client ever noticed this as an area of concern.

Chapter 4:

Why Cost Can Be An Elusive Selection Tool

Cost is always a factor that is considered when selecting the lot, the home design, the architect, and the builder. But, as we mentioned in the previous chapter, it is just **one** aspect of the overall factors considered. Yet, so many times, we see clients make the big mistake of making cost the <u>primary</u> selection tool. In the homebuilding industry, making a decision primarily based on cost, can be a very dangerous selection tool. This chapter is dedicated to discussing the complexities of price and how you can ensure you're making an apples to apples comparison.

1. Apples to Apples

You will see the concept of 'Apples to Apples' repeated throughout this book because, far too many times, we've seen homeowners make decisions based on pricing or specifications that were <u>not</u> apples to apples. The easiest way to ensure you are comparing apples to apples is to begin with a <u>detailed</u> set of specifications. We discuss this concept in detail in Chapter 17.

Here is one example:

> Jim and Linda were determined to build a house with a budget of $1.5M. They met with an architect who drew up their dream home with all of the designs they desired. Although a preliminary budget was discussed with the architect, the specifications were vague and the architect advised them that detailed specifications would need to developed and reviewed with the builder.

We met with Jim and Linda and reviewed their drawings. Since they had not spent the time or money to create a detailed set of specifications with the architect, we provided a price that included many of the materials and specifications we felt would be commonly used for similarly styled homes and budgets. Our estimate was that the home would cost approximately $1.85M to build. Meanwhile, they received a bid from another builder for $1.55M and wanted to know why there was such a price difference – a legitimate question.

We offered to review the specifications, where it was determined that our bid included an allowance for commercial-grade appliances such as Thermador or Wolf whereas the other builder used a mid-level GE line and this example of "incomparable allowances and specifications" was prevalent through all the other pricing and selections, causing an obvious discrepancy in price, value and overall quality.

Now, while it was not a problem to use GE appliances if that is what the client preferred, it certainly did not provide an apples to apples comparison. Meanwhile, the client expected upper-end selections, so this assumption and inconsistency should have been a big red flag. Instead, they approached the other builder to discuss the discrepancies. The builder indicated that he could provide all of the *higher-end selections for the same price.* So, we shook hands with the client and parted ways, amicably of course.

While persistence can be a good thing, it does not override the theory that 'you get what you pay for.' They ultimately signed a contract with the builder for the $1.55M price they had in mind. Unfortunately, that was not the end of the story. About eight months into their project, and after $1M had been drawn down from their construction loan, the house was only about *half-way finished*. By this time, they realized that there was no way the house could be completed for the remaining $550,000. The selected builder (who coincidentally only had about 5 years of experience) informed them that he could not continue the project without additional funds. The bank would not release any more funds until the previous phases had been completed. So, the entire project, half-way done, came to a complete stand-still. What a mess!

2. Too Good to be True

The saying "It's Too Good to be True" is worth its weight in gold. If one builder's price is 5-8% different than another's – it's too good to be true or there is something wrong. The reality is that if all things are equal (and this is a BIG if), each builder's pricing structure should be relatively close. As we will discuss later, you can avoid a lot of issues, by contracting an architect or builder to prepare a complete set of detailed design specifications [see Ch. 17].

When detailed specifications aren't provided, some builders will try to cut corners on price, just to get the business and make it up later. They may provide vague specifications or offer to 'do it for a better price.' In most of these cases, the builder cannot finish the project, goes out of business, or the homeowner ends up struggling to find the cash to make up the difference. This reality often hits somewhere in the middle of the construction process when you have few options – either during selections, half-way through the construction process, etc. When your builder tells you that everything is included in their price, be cautious.

3. Vague Specifications

When obtaining or reviewing the pricing and specifications, you want to be extremely careful about any builder package that has vague or general specifications. This is why we reiterate throughout this book, that you should work with an architect or builder to create <u>detailed</u> design specifications. It is virtually impossible to compare apples to apples or stay within a budget when specifications have not been clearly outlined. Vague specifications leave a lot of room for interpretation, cost variation, and substitution (often with lower quality products). Whether you're working with an architect, or directly with the builder, it is critical to have detailed specifications so that you have a clear understanding of exactly what type of quality, materials, and finishes you will have in your home. This process requires considerable time and resources but saves the homeowner, the builder and the architect from uncertainty and confusion. You will likely pay either the architect or the builder a design fee to prepare a detailed list of specifications. This is money well spent, regardless of the builder you choose. Here are a few reasons why:

One small example that can cause variables in pricing is a simple matter, like selecting the paint for your home. Now, it may or may not matter to you which quality of paint you select. That decision is yours alone and your builder, architect or interior designer can help guide you as to the pros/cons of this decision. However, by not selecting the paint, you are opening yourself up to apples/oranges bids or quotes. For example, one builder may price in a standard 'builder grade' paint whereas another builder may select higher-end quality paint. Sherwin Williams Emerald series, which is a high-end finish selected by many interior designers, may cost $55/gallon while Sherwin Williams Pro-Coat may cost as little as $15/gallon. As with most materials, the larger the home, the more the cost differential. The homeowner may or may not have a preference, but the differences between specifications should be carefully reviewed and discussed as part of the budgeting process. A quality custom luxury home builder typically recommends products that are consistent with the type of home they are building. Again, there is no right or wrong selection, but the specification needs to be clear so that you are comparing apples to apples. These small decisions and choices start to create vast price differences between one quote and another and you don't want to sacrifice your selections, without knowing that you are making that choice. Vague specifications allow the builder to choose, versus you.

On the other hand, it takes considerable time and effort for a builder to provide you a thoroughly prepared estimate with detailed specifications. This is why many builders charge a design fee to create detailed specifications. An architect may also be used to facilitate this process, but again a design fee will likely be charged, as the time and effort are not insignificant. However, this design fee is irrelevant when it helps you ensure that you are comparing apples to apples and assuring that you are not sacrificing quality without a conscious decision to do so. If your builder's bid is overly general, buyer beware.

> We met with a couple, Michelle and Brian, to discuss their dream home. We discussed their preferences and budget. We showed them a variety of photos of various builds, designs, and finishes to understand their expectations. Following this discussion, we prepared our estimate for review with them. They had questions about our estimate and were concerned because they had received a 'comparable bid' from another builder for a substantially lower cost. So, we asked if we could help them compare the two estimates side by side and ensure they were comparing apples to apples. They agreed. What we found is that the other builder's 'comparable estimate' was lacking, to say the least! Not only

did it include vague specifications, but in many cases, the finishes and allowances were not included, or even comparable, to what they expected of a luxury home.

Here is a list of *some of the differences* between the Mueller specifications and the 'comparable' vague specifications provided by the other builder:

Table 1.1

	Mueller (Builder A)	Comparable Bid (Builder B)
1.	Our estimating binder was **44** pages.	The competitor's package was **12** pages.
2.	Based on our in-depth discussions with the client, we specified custom tile work in each of the bathrooms for the floors, baths, and showers.	The 'comparable' bid had *vague specifications* and the homeowner determined that the estimate only included shower pans and pre-fabricated tubs. In addition, one powder room was completely *left out of the specification package altogether.*
3.	Our bid included exposed wood barn beams in the great room.	No beams were specified in the 'comparable' bid.
4.	Our bid included a $100,000 landscape/hardscape package, including sidewalks and a driveway.	The 'comparable' bid included sidewalks and a driveway with no additional landscape/hardscape package.
5.	James Hardie plank siding was specified in our package.	The 'comparable' bid included *vague specifications* and the allowance provided only covered the cost of vinyl siding.

It was apparent to us that the 'comparable' builder, in this situation, did not have an in-depth conversation about the desired specifications and may or may not have intentionally left them vague to meet a certain budget. The client was unaware of the vast difference between the specifications. While a homeowner certainly has the option to choose the quality or selections they deem appropriate, one should be very careful that they are comparing apples to apples and building the type of home with the kind of materials they expect. You can also see that there are areas where a home can be value-engineered if a client is budget-minded, such as in Item #4 above where the exterior landscaping package could be significantly scaled-down if the homeowner so desires.

Providing pricing with vague specifications is unconscionable, in our minds, and certainly not building the type of transparent, credible and trusting relationship for which we strive. As a matter of fact, this type of pricing creates just the opposite, for the industry as a whole. These clients felt as though this builder was trying to pull one over on them, creating distrust and a lack of confidence. If you sense your builder is being vague or giving you specifications that are incomplete we urge you to consider choosing another builder.

4. Insufficient Allowances

One of the most common ways that an unscrupulous builder will present a price that is too good to be true, is to knowingly or unknowingly include allowances that are insufficient to complete your home as expected. Of course, you won't realize this until you are knee-deep in the project and the change orders start coming through.

The allowances provided by your builder should be based on the discussions you've had and typically aligned with the finish and specifications throughout the remainder of the home unless purposefully specified otherwise. You should have a good sense of what your allowances will buy. Vague specifications open the door wide for insufficient allowances, so if you notice this occurring, be very wary.

5. Value Engineering

Often, our clients come to us, looking for an architect to assist them with the design of the home and we have a wealth of resources to help match them with an architect who is capable of serving their needs. Other times, a client has already met with an architect to draft the original designs. We work with either scenario, but it's important for a client to be aware of the fact that an architect is not typically responsible for knowing current material costs and/or adhering to the final budget. Therefore, the designs may need to be reviewed and/or value-engineered to ensure that the home and specifications align with the customer's budget.

In one such case, one couple came to us with a beautiful home design which they had invested a substantial amount of time, money, and thought. While the designs were gorgeous, the specifications far exceeded the client's budget. After further discussion, we were able to recommend several areas for consideration. One recommendation was to scale down some of the exterior hardscaping specifications which reduced the budget by about $30,000. In another area, we were able to modify the window specifications by another $20,000. Ultimately, after a few minor adjustments and compromises, a working plan was agreed upon and the project was able to move forward, at the desired budget. Communication is the key when making these types of adjustments to ensure the clients' goals and budgets are aligned.

As demonstrated in the examples above, value engineering may be required to get your final numbers closer to your budget. However, these discussions cannot take place with *vague specifications* or without correlation to the appropriate budget line items. Vague specifications would not have allowed us to make alternative recommendations. The client may have had one type of finish in mind, but without clear specifications, the difference between what's on paper and what is quoted can be two different things, causing confusion and frustration before the project begins.

This example also highlights the importance of the builder and architect having a collaborative work relationship which we will discuss further in Part 2 of this book.

You see, at the end of the day, it simply costs what it costs to build your home. Materials, labor costs, and even profit margins are fairly consistent so, if you see one builder's pricing substantially lower than another – this is a RED FLAG ALERT!

Authors Comments:

The bottom line is that while the cost is certainly an important consideration when building a luxury home, there are other factors that can directly influence costs, time, and the overall building experience so, one should be very careful about selecting a builder based solely on price.

Chapter 5:

How Many Builders Should I Get to Price My House?

Everyone wants to ensure they are getting a fair price, and many homeowners think they need to get bids to ensure that. There is nothing wrong with this concept, but if you select a quality builder to start, the traditional bid process is not as important as ensuring you have a great working relationship with the builder who you will partner with for the coming months/years.

We have discussed the importance of researching and choosing your builder wisely. So, while you are perfectly entitled to send your designs out to 10 builders if you choose, we feel that carefully selecting 2-3 builders is ideal. This allows you to do your homework - thoroughly research your builder and determine if you can build a good working relationship with them. It also allows your builder to focus on the complex estimating process for projects that are more likely suited for them.

Speaking from personal experience, if I know I'm on a bid with 9 other contractors, I am going to focus my efforts where I can be most effective and that's not going to be bidding on a project that is likely to be an apples to *oranges* game of *bidding*. Not to mention, there is a tremendous amount of time invested in the estimating process which could be a waste of valuable resources. I'm also not going to bother my past clients with providing references or taking phone calls from prospects who may not be serious.

Before you proceed, remember:

1. Invest in creating a detailed set of design specifications to ensure you're comparing apples to apples.

2. How do each of the builders <u>and</u> their businesses stack up?

3. Builder/architect collaboration is key

Chapter 6:

Managing Expectations

1. Identifying Expectations

Expectations are defined as, "a belief that someone will or should achieve something." But, it's hard to achieve those expectations if you don't know what they are. That is why it is important for you and your builder to have a heart to heart conversation about your expectations and, as with any long-term relationship, be willing to meet in the middle when necessary. After all, we all have different personality types and ways in which we communicate. So, it's important for both the builder and client to understand each other's expectations and adjust accordingly. This is not always easy.

A few years back, we worked with a businessman who owned a large accounting firm. His background and personality style was extremely detail oriented, data-driven, and precise. That is obviously what made him a very successful accountant. We recognized that he would enjoy the data and details surrounding the building process, but we also knew that the fluid, sometimes unpredictable process of building a home, could be challenging. You see, in his business, there were no *flexible* timelines. His expectation for precision was what made him a great accountant, but not necessarily realistic, when it comes to building a home. So, we discussed the scenarios that would impact the proposed construction schedule, such as permitting, weather, and other factors. These conversations were important to identify and manage his expectations.

The construction process began, and we provided detailed reports at each meeting, specifically about the budget and finances, which met his expectations wonderfully. Things were going well until winter came and foul weather really impacted the schedule and progress – something totally beyond our control. We adjusted the project timelines and of course, the expectations had to be reset. These changes were challenging because he just wasn't accustomed to working in that kind of environment. Eventually, we got through the winter and, even though the construction schedule shifted a number of times, the construction was completed in a timely manner. But it was important that we had anticipated these challenges and worked to manage his expectations, weekly. Once he realized that we were doing all we could, his anxiety eased and the overall experience was a good one. This story illustrates the need for identifying expectations and clear communication throughout the construction process, between the builder and the client.

2. Excellence or Perfection?

Another great way to establish client expectations is to take a tour of a previously built home and discuss the construction methods, finishes, craftsmanship, efficiencies, and other details. If the home meets your expectations, great! If you want or expect something more, that's fine too but there should be a clear discussion to understand and manage expectations up front.

It's also worth noting that when we talk about expectations, we are operating under the assumption that when you build a luxury custom home, a high level of quality is expected. But, to further manage expectations, we really need to address the difference between excellence and perfection.

There are a number of different explanations for excellence vs. perfection. Let's look at the definitions of each to understand better:

Excellence: the quality of being outstanding or extremely good

Perfection: the action or process of improving something until it is *faultless*

"People" build homes and "people" are not perfect or faultless. So, it's important to understand expectations and the difference between a perfect home and a home built with excellence. Vince Lombardi said, **"Perfection is not attainable, but if we chase perfection, we can catch excellence."** That perfectly sums up our belief and approach to custom luxury home building. Make sure that you and your builder are aligned with regard to your expectations and that those expectations are humanly possible to achieve. This will add to your overall experience, especially if you are working with a builder who strives for excellence while managing your expectations for perfection.

Chapter 7:

Builder References

As discussed earlier in this book, references are an important part of the builder selection process. A builder should be able to give you multiple recent references *for recent builds* and even some older references. If they don't want to provide more than 1-2 because they don't want you to 'bother' their clients, beware! Most happy clients are willing to share a few minutes of their experience. We have provided a *Questions to Ask Builder References (Appendix Checklist #2)* that can be used to facilitate this process.

It's important to realize that one builder can't be all things to all people. Each builder will have strengths and limitations. Some builders excel at producing a modest home with modern conveniences while others will excel at producing a home equipped with every detail and luxury. You want to find the builder who excels at building the type of home **you** are looking to build. As discussed in previous chapters, you'll want to ensure they have good references along with experience, excellence, and integrity. A reputable builder knows their strengths and weaknesses and is not afraid to be transparent.

Remember, the selection of your builder and the relationship you establish is paramount to the entire process, and references can help you ensure you're making the best decision for you and the type of home you want to build.

Chapter 8:

What Kind of Warranty Do You Offer?

When evaluating potential builders, it is important to understand the type of warranty your builder offers. You are likely going to be interacting with your builder, about your home, for years to come. So, you'll want to be certain that not only are they prepared to respond to your requests, but that they have a warranty policy or process in place to support you for years to come.

Since warranties vary by builder and manufacturer's often change their warranties, we do not outline any specific policies here but advise you to understand the difference between one builder's policies and another.

It's also a good time to understand how the builder handles issues, even after the house is built. It's also a pretty good indicator of the builder's overall philosophy and business model. Be sure to include this as a conversation point in your list of reference questions. There are bound to be problems along the way, but the sign of a great company is how they respond to those problems, long after the sale is complete.

Chapter 9:

Before You Buy That Lot...

We often receive calls from folks who have been looking at Lots and have narrowed their choices down to two or three options. The Realtor may be a good guide, but the Realtor is not responsible for determining whether or not the house you'd like to build <u>can</u> actually be built on the Lot you are selecting. So, instead of buying the Lot first, we highly recommend getting your Realtor to help you nail down a few options and then using a collaborative team approach including the architect, builder and/ or civil engineer to make the final decision. If you've never purchased a Lot, this can help you to avoid serious issues. Here is a story to demonstrate why collaboration is so important.

A few years ago, we were approached by Joanie and Dave. They had purchased a Lot in an area that was very desirable and paid a premium for the land. After it was purchased, they began working on plans for their dream home. They were very excited by the time they met with us to get started building their dream home.

However, when we visited the property, we were immediately concerned about the topography of the land, set back requirements in relation to nearby homes, and well/septic requirements. The Lot was also located near a tributary which carried with it even more restrictions. We concluded that the location was not suitable for the <u>size and type</u> of home they wanted to build. They had spent a tremendous amount of time, money and effort and now they had a very hard decision to make – move forward building a different type of home, that was not their dream home, or selling the property and starting over.

This is an unfortunate, but not uncommon, story. The moral is that if you are looking for a Lot or land, be sure to have your team selected, and on standby, so that they can help you determine if the Lot is the right fit for the home you want to build. Alternatively, having flexibility with your dream home concept will provide more alternatives, if you've already bought the Lot.

In addition, if you purchase a piece of land, primarily based on price, you may discover unexpected issues later on. Here are some things to consider:

- Permitting and impact fees vary by county and must be factored into the overall cost/budget.

- Will additional clearing or grading be required? Site work and fill dirt can increase your cost by thousands.

- Does the Lot require a septic system, mounded system, or have access to public utilities? The cost variables can be substantial.

- Is the property located in/near the waterfront? A variety of additional considerations including critical area requirements, impervious surface calculations, and impact fees must be factored into the overall cost and time schedule.

- Does the property need to have a site development plan approved by the county? This can add significant time and money to the overall budget.

Of course, these are just some of the issues that must be considered. Meeting with an experienced architect, builder, or engineer *before* you buy the Lot will save you time and money in the long run and help you make an informed decision.

Chapter 10:

Should I Hire an Independent Building Inspector?

Some homeowners choose to hire an independent building inspector to oversee the construction of their new home. There is nothing inherently right or wrong with this decision except that if you are hiring a competent builder with a great reputation, whom you trust, you should not need to incur the cost of an independent building inspector. Keep in mind that most jurisdictions also require regular inspections, throughout the construction process. Let's look at both sides of this coin.

On one hand, if the homeowner is concerned with the builder's capabilities, you could certainly understand why hiring an independent building inspector makes sense. But we would first ask why you would want to hire a builder you don't trust or feel is capable?

On the other hand, let's assume that you are confident in the builder, but want to hire an independent building inspector just to ensure that all the I's are dotted and the T's are crossed. We have worked with homeowners that live out of the area and want to have someone watch over the process, on their behalf. If this is what makes you completely comfortable with the entire building process – the decision and expense are yours, so it's completely up to you!

Regardless of the reason, it is important to ensure that your intent is clear with both the builder and the inspector so that the overall process and the builder/inspector relationship is not adversarial. There is no benefit to hiring an inspector *who feels the need to justify his fee* and interferes with the construction process, complicates the communication process, or provides unwarranted criticism. Everyone should be working together, throughout the construction process, to create a beautiful quality home within the time frames and budgets provided. That is the ultimate goal.

If you choose to hire a building inspector, have a team meeting with all parties, upfront, before the process begins. Outline the goals and oversight you require so that everyone is on the same page. In this way, the builder and inspector can build a good working relationship that provides you the level of comfort you desire.

Authors Comments:
If your motivation for hiring a building inspector is driven out of concern about the builder and/or his practices, you should probably be questioning your builder selection, not hiring a building inspector.

Part 2

BUDGETING & FINANCING

Chapter 11:

Financing Options

If you have unlimited financial resources, then you can skip this chapter altogether, but if not, you'll want to know what options you have to consider for the financing of your home. Some homeowners have cash for a portion of the project but take advantage of low-interest rates to finance the rest. Some homeowners finance the entire project, while still others pay cash.

The first thing you will want to do is select a lender **with construction experience**. This is not the time or place for an online loan. A good place to start is by asking your builder who they have typically worked with in the past. Just like the vendors and sub-contractors that a builder works with, the builder has likely developed trusted relationships with local banks. Remember, the loan is a critical part of the home building process and you want the bank and the builder to work well together. You also want a financial institution that can process draws and the associated inspections in a timely manner, to keep your project on-schedule. Many local and community banks have construction lending departments. Construction lending is a unique niche and you'll want to make sure your loan officer has experience in this area. Use the *Questions About Financing Checklist (Appendix Checklist #4)* to help facilitate your selection.

Keep in mind that just because you qualify for a $3M loan doesn't mean you should spend $3M. You want to ensure you're living within your means, as discussed in Chapter 12, and that the payment is affordable for you.

The financing industry is ever-changing, as are the programs available. So, we won't explore specific options here, but the bottom line is that you will want to be sure you are working with an **experienced** construction lender who can guide you to the best programs and structure a loan that meets your specific needs.

While some builders offer "builder financing," the more common approach, when building a custom home, is for the borrower to obtain financing through a local lender. Construction loans are handled much the same as a regular home loan, except that there are often two elements to the loan:

1. A loan to be used during the construction of the home and then

2. A permanent loan once the home is completed.

Due to the complexity of the construction lending process, the draw process, and other factors, the rates may be slightly higher during construction. Again, having an experienced construction lender is key. Your lender will conduct routine inspections as the home is built and typically require certain items to be completed before releasing any draws or payments to the builder.

It will also be very important to discuss and understand the implications of change orders during the building process. If, for example, the kitchen allowance was $50,000 but you decide to add a special feature or design element during construction, which puts the kitchen over budget by $5,000 – the lender, you, and the builder need to understand where the additional funds are coming from for the costs of that change order. We discuss change orders in further detail in Chapter 27.

Types of Loans

Generally speaking, there are three types of home construction loans used in custom home building.

- **Lot Loan** – A Lot loan is different than a construction loan because it only pays for the land that the construction will take place on. It is also generally a short-term loan, with the assumption that a home will be built on the property in the near future. Some lenders will transfer a Lot loan into a construction loan. The terms of a Lot loan vary by lender with some offering interest-only loans or interest and principal.

- **Construction/Perm** – This type of loan is the more common or preferred method for many homeowners. In this scenario, you borrow money to pay for the Lot (if not already owned) and the construction – and there is only one loan closing. One loan closing provides benefits because it often reduces the fees associated with two separate loans. In addition, you are typically able to lock in the long-term rate (or a rate range) for the permanent loan.

During the construction, you pay interest only on the outstanding balance. Typically, the rate is variable during construction and will go up or down based on the prime rate. The lender escrows the funds and releases them after various phases of construction are complete. After construction is complete and a Certificate of Occupancy is obtained, this type of loan is often converted into a permanent mortgage. Some lenders will lock-in a mortgage rate or a range when construction begins. Most lenders require a 20% down payment based on the completed value of the home, but each lender has a variety of loan programs and down payment options, based on what is currently available in the lending market.

- **Stand-Alone Construction** – This type of loan establishes a loan for the Lot (if not already owned) and construction costs. When you are ready to move in, you will receive another loan to pay off any remaining construction debt and to provide a permanent mortgage for your new home.

This type of loan may be desirable for those that have an existing home, perhaps with equity, that they want to use as credit towards their down payment. However, this type of loan typically requires two closings, which means two sets of fees – first on the construction loan, and then on the permanent mortgage. Rarely are you able to lock in a rate, so you are subject to whatever the rates are, once the house is completed. In addition, you will need to re-qualify for the second loan so it's important to understand your options and keep credit and spending in check, during the construction of your home. This can prove challenging to some, so a good lender is the key!

One thing to remember is that with both the Construction/Perm loan and the Stand-Alone Construction loan, the loan amount is determined before construction begins. While allowances may be provided in your construction contract, any variance or additional costs would need to be paid out of pocket. Your experienced lender will be able to answer specific questions about down payment options, draw schedule, rates, fees, and more.

Chapter 12:

Building Within Your Means

Your builder is your guide for construction and your lender should be your guide for financing. Be upfront with your lender about your financial goals, down payment, cash available, monthly payment, etc. No matter how beautiful the home, no one enjoys living in a home that they really can't afford.

We have already talked about the importance of having the builder involved in the design process to ensure that your budget and vision are aligned. But, even after you have your concepts on paper, there are still a number of decisions that must be made and all of these decisions can impact your budget, your financing, and your monthly payment. Depending on your financial situation, it's important to ensure this part of the process doesn't run away from you.

Let's look at a story that exemplifies this perfectly. Have you ever gone to buy a car? You decide on the type or model and a general budget – let's say $50,000. You do some research on the web and determine that $50,000 is a reasonable budget for your needs. You then venture out to the local dealers to drive and compare. Upon arrival, you notice that many of the cars on the lot have upgrades and features you had not originally considered. After driving the car, you decide to add a few options for an additional $10,000. After all, if you're going to spend $50,000 on a car, you want all of the bells and whistles! Suddenly, you realize that you've added 20% to your initial budget, bringing the cost of the vehicle to $60,000 + taxes, title & tags. This amount puts the car well beyond your budget and perhaps even "your means."

This same type of story often happens when we begin the home building process, sometimes exponentially. You want to maximize the features and benefits of your dream home but the options and selections start to take on a life (and budget) of their own. Often, a homeowner gets so excited that they say, "Well, we are only building our dream home once, and we really want to have this or that."

Your builder's job is to ensure that your home can be completed for the budget you've provided. This requires some honest conversations during the process, about the changes you request, and how they will be paid for. We believe it's important to be clear about your budget, and as discussed earlier, leave yourself a bit of 'wiggle room' for the upgrades and unexpected expenses that will no doubt occur during the construction process.

Most importantly, you want to build a home that you feel good about walking into every day. You want to be comfortable with the financial aspects of the building process. You do not want to complicate the process or compromise your overall experience, with a home that is beyond your means.

Authors Comments:
Your builder is your guide for construction and your lender should be your guide for financing.
Be sure to choose a lender with extensive experience in construction lending.

Chapter 13:

Establishing A Budget

Once you decide to build a custom luxury home, the adrenaline, emotions, and excitement may drive you to the nearest builder or architect's office to start designing your dream home. STOP! You may have heard the quote, "Suppose one of you wants to build a tower. Won't you first sit down and estimate the costs?" So, too it's important to understand financing and costs before jumping into the design of a home. Why sit down and start designing a $5M home, if your budget is closer to $2.5M?

Establishing a realistic budget for your custom home is a critical component of the home building process and should be done as early on, in the process, as possible.

There are many items your builder will help ensure you include, but a few are the costs for the Lot, site preparation, permitting, construction, detailed specifications, landscaping and more. Once these numbers are finalized, we recommend adding a 5-8% surplus for 'wiggle room'– the areas where you want or need to spend a little more, as construction progresses. This may include upgrading a particular feature of the home, or to cover unexpected expenses that arise, such as when additional engineering is required, after soil analysis. Either way, by including a cushion, you'll be sure you have the cash or financing to cover additional expenses associated with the build.

If you are working with an architect, it's important to be sure the builder is part of the budget and design process to ensure the home meets your expectations while maintaining a budget that is aligned with your finances. Architects will often recommend 2-3 comparable builders you can interview and the budget estimates should be based on detailed specifications.

Your builder and architect should be doing everything possible to maximize your budget and overall investment – creating efficiencies and value engineering where necessary while providing the luxuries and creature comforts you desire. Sometimes a homeowner will "hold back" let's say $50,000. Halfway through the project, the homeowner informs the builder that they've decided to add another $50,000 to add on another room, add a pool feature, or other elements. This may cost significant time and money since the design process may need to be revisited and the construction schedule will have to be revised.

The bottom line is that you should trust and have a good relationship with your builder and architect and be transparent about your budget. As the construction progresses, you're both on the same page and trying to utilize those funds wisely, for the things you really desire. Ultimately, the building process should be a partnership with the end goal of providing you a home that you enjoy and is financially affordable for you.

Chapter 14:

Fixed Price or Cost Plus?

When you choose to build your home, there are two types of construction contracts used in the construction industry. There are pros and cons to each, for both the buyer and the builder. Let's examine the two types:

Fixed Price

An agreement where the builder is contracted to construct the home at a set price. The buyer often likes this contract because there is a set amount (unless change orders are requested) for the entire construction process. Fixed price contracts provide clients a clear budgeting process, provided the specifications and allowances are clearly stated. In this model, the builder assumes the risk for any material and labor price fluctuations.

Completed drawings with clear specifications are essential to the fixed price process. Here is where we **strongly** advise you to contract either your builder or architect to work with you to provide detailed specifications. Detailed specifications ensure you're comparing apples to apples and preferences will be priced into the project. There may be allowances for some items, but detailed specifications make sure those allowances are in line with your expectations and preferences. We discuss the consistency of design and selections later in this book as well.

Pros – the Fixed Price model provides a relative certainty of costs, adherence to a defined budget, and the builder is incentivized to efficiently procure and execute the project.

Cons – the Fixed Price model means that the homeowner must make most of the selections in advance before final pricing can be provided and work can begin.

Cost Plus

An agreement where the builder is contracted to construct the home at actual costs plus a pre-agreed upon fee (to cover overhead, administration, and profit). If the buyer wants certainty with the final cost, without variation (other than change orders), this is not the ideal model. This type of arrangement is used when the homeowner or architect wants to be intimately involved with the entire construction process, making decisions and design selections, as the project progresses vs. upfront. This process is completely transparent with the builder providing all the details and associated costs to the client, with a fixed margin added to each for the building and administration of the home.

Pros - Cost Plus may be more appropriate for the client who has a more flexible budget. It may also be preferable when the plans and specs are not finalized and it makes sense to begin construction without complete details. For the client who wants the building experience to evolve, and to make decisions as the project progresses, perhaps with the guidance of interior designer or architect, this is often the method preferred.

Cons - However, keep in mind, that the cost-plus model will leave the budget much more open-ended.

There is also more paperwork involved with this process, as an added layer of accounting is required because costs are consolidated and accounted for on a monthly basis and presented to the owner for monthly payment.

Most luxury custom builders can accommodate either approach, but make your decision with a clear understanding of the pros/cons.

Chapter 15:

Understanding the Cost Per Square Foot

Many people ask the question, "What is your cost per square foot (CPSF)?" While this question may be relatively easy to answer when building a production or semi-custom home, there is just no easy answer when building a custom or luxury home. There are so many variables to consider. Luxury homes, in particular, include so many details and customized features that are specifically designed for each homeowner and their lifestyle. Let's consider a few examples.

Below is an example of two different homes we built in recent years with approximately the same square footage, but a <u>big difference in cost per square footage</u>. There is a vast difference between these two homes, based on the homeowner's preferences and budget. Although this chart provides limited detail, you'll notice the selections, specifications, and the level of quality and finish desired are vastly different. Please note that the homeowner dictates all of these areas, which affect the budget and overall value of the home. These are two extreme examples and there could be variations anywhere in between.

	Homeowner Smith	Homeowner Johnson
Square Foot	4700	5000
CPSF	$510/sf	$165/sf
Total Budget	$2,400,000 (Excluding Lot costs)	$825,000 (Excluding Lot costs)

	Homeowner Smith	Homeowner Johnson
Site Work	$92,500	$45,000
	(1-acre site, clearing, long drive-way, utilities, fill dirt, septic, storm-water management)	(1/2-acre site, no clear-ing, short driveway, no fill dirt, no stormwater mgmt.)
Hardscape	$315,000	$10,000
	(pool, entrance monuments, 2500 sf wet-laid stone for deck-ing on structural concrete with frost-heave protection, landscape architect designed plantings)	(modest planting package with no exterior features)
Home Cost	$2,000,000	$770,000
	Extensive custom handcrafted millwork and cabinetry through-out, specialty in-laid wood flooring, custom stair treads and railings, commissioned lighting and high-end plumbing fixtures, steam/body wash shower, highest quality design selections, smart home automation, complex archi-tecture.	Simplistic moldings, millwork, stock cabinetry, standard hardwood and carpeted areas, standard lighting and plumbing fixtures, basic architec-tural style.
Resources	Architect Landscape Architect Interior Designer	None

Here are some other examples that show how the cost per square foot is completely driven by the customer's preferences and varies widely.

- Recently, we built a 14,000 square foot home on a wooded lot. It included a 1,100-gallon saltwater fish tank, an 800 square foot home theatre room, smart home automation, and a separate two-story piano room designed exclusively for the homeowner's baby grand piano. The stair railings and flooring were one-of-a-kind pieces of artwork, made specifically for this homeowner's unique tastes. The CPSF for this home was $325.00.

- Another home, we built a few years ago, was approximately 6,000 square feet. The homeowner desired a lot of open space for entertaining families. The open space and modern design required much less millwork, cabinetry, and detail than some other homes. While the home featured many personalized and custom features, there was nothing intricate or over the top. The CPSF for this home was $245.00.

- Another home, we recently completed, was approximately 5,000 square feet with every bell and whistle you can imagine. Custom built-ins were featured in almost every room, tray ceilings, a large chef kitchen and rare flooring materials were included throughout. In addition, the home included an extensive hardscaping, landscaping, and pool package. The CPSF for this home was $515.00.

Another variable that largely impacts a home's cost is the site work and preparation of the land. There are large variations of cost based on topography, if the Lot is wooded or cleared, length of the driveway, stormwater management, sediment control, jurisdiction, building permit fees, impact fees, and more.

With these examples, you can easily see why a luxury custom home really can't be given a *standard* cost per square foot price. The price of your home will be largely determined by:

- **Style & Complexity** – What kind of architectural details are specified? How many levels is the home? Are there intricate elements of design?

- **Quality & Level of Finish** – Do you want unique one-of-a-kind materials and selections? Do you want the top of the line, or moderate grade appliances and flooring?

- **Size & Scope** – A 4,000 square foot home (conditioned area) may include a two-car unheated garage; whereas a 6,000 square foot home may include a three-car heated garage. With more size often come luxuries like multiple porches and decks, a larger outdoor area or pool, etc.

Your lifestyle, preferences, and expectations will largely impact the price per square foot. We recommend including a reputable builder _early_ in the design phase. If you are budget-conscious, you'll want to ensure that your design expectations are compatible with your budget. An experienced and reputable builder can offer suggestions, and work collaboratively with your architect, on ways to value-engineer your project to ensure your expectations and budget are aligned.

Chapter 16:

Factors That Can Influence Costs

There are a number of outside factors that influence the cost of a home, beyond you or your builder's control. The market, inflation, supplies and even foreign trade relations can have an impact on costs. In the early 2000s, for example, domestic production of raw materials could not keep up with the booming real estate and construction industry. Production for materials such as drywall, concrete and other raw materials was inflated 2-3 times higher than normal. Overseas manufacturers supplemented domestic production, but for a much higher cost. For those that **had** to have their home built, the costs were <u>not</u> negotiable – these projects had to be completed.

As discussed previously, structural design and architectural complexities have a great influence on costs too. Site work and topography can also have a major impact on costs.

Large scale disasters often can have an effect on the laws of supply and demand too! For example, after a hurricane or other natural disaster, demand will often surge for materials and prices may be much higher.

But, the area where we've seen the most cost variation, is in the area of "**_allowances_**." This is such a critical area of the 'cost' process, that we dedicate Chapter 17 to a full discussion of estimates and allowances. We have seen this as an area of discrepancy and unfortunately abuse, in the industry. Don't be fooled by a "lower sticker price" without being educated and aware of the implications. The bottom line is that, as we've stated elsewhere in this book, if you are truly comparing apples to apples, one builder's cost and price structure should not be more than 5-8% from another's. If it is, then red flags should go up all around! Stay tuned for more on that discussion.

Chapter 17:

Estimating, Specifications & Allowances (ESA)

As mentioned in the opening of this book, we have been in the construction industry for over 40 years and we have seen the good, bad and the ugly. In our opinion, when it comes to custom home building, **the Estimating, Specifications, and Allowances (also referred to as ESA) process of home building is the primary area of misinterpretation, misunderstanding, and miscommunication.** Let's consider why this is such a critical area to understand.

For many consumers, the process of building a custom home and choosing a builder comes down to the numbers. Although we have provided many other factors we believe are just as important to consider, for some people, it just comes down to price. While there is nothing inherently wrong with being cost-conscious, it's important to fully understand the ESA process because it can cause major price variances.

We have met with hundreds of clients over the years. We have certainly met with homeowners who 'got a lower bid' or 'a bid that was significantly less than ours' and chose to go with another builder. In some cases, this worked out. But, in the overwhelming majority of cases, there was something wrong and it usually came down to the ESA process.

You can opt to pay a design fee to an architect or builder to create a detailed set of specifications, but <u>you must have detailed specifications to get an accurate 'apples to apples' estimate</u>. We believe there are no cutting corners in this regard.

1. Estimating

We believe that any estimate you consider should be thoroughly detailed. As discussed earlier in this book, we have seen many homeowners get several price quotes, that are not equal, and get lured down a slippery slope. The level of detail included in an estimate has a direct correlation to your home building experience. You'll want to consider how the estimates are performed and what level of detail is provided. As you recall, in the example we shared in Chapter 4, *Builder A* fully estimated every line item in the budget or obtained an estimate from a vendor or sub-contractor whereas *Builder B* went off historical data to estimate the project, with fewer details, lower quality selections and limited accounting. As you consider the estimate, there are two additional areas that will factor into an apples to apples comparison: Specifications and Allowances.

2. Specifications

Just as a builder cannot possibly give you pricing without a detailed set of drawings, so too, a builder can not possibly give you accurate pricing on the cost to build your home, <u>without detailed specifications</u>. This is often a timely and thought-provoking process that requires a considerable amount of time and effort. For example, do you prefer:

- Vinyl siding or Hardi-plank siding

- Custom hand-made cabinetry or stock cabinetry

- Standard oak stair treads or custom wood stair treads that match the rest of your flooring

- The list goes on and on

It is these personal preferences and details that truly make a custom home uniquely yours. In addition, a detailed estimate provides benchmarks for every single item so that as you make your final selections, you will understand any cost variations.

This level of detail provides a much better home building experience, for a number of reasons.

First, you have taken the time to carefully consider the design and quality you want to utilize in every aspect of your home. Second, when you are considering design changes, you understand the associated costs and can make a very informed decision. For example, sometimes a homeowner will agree to one set of specifications during the design process, but as the home building project progresses, they may decide they want something different. Perhaps you chose a mid-range lighting package with a nickel finish during the design specifications phase. But, during the actual building process, you realize that the lighting in the great room could be enhanced with a different style or design, perhaps to be used as a focal point. Because you created detailed specifications at the outset of the project, you know that the lighting budget included in your original specifications was $20,000. But, to add the new lighting features you desire will cost an additional $6000. You can easily understand the $6000 cost difference so that when a change order is processed, you have a frame of reference for what you were originally budgeted and what you are now spending. Or, perhaps you choose to upgrade all of the lighting to a different design with a rubbed bronze finish, and the cost to upgrade the entire lighting package is determined to be $30,000. You now can make an educated decision about whether or not this the direction you want to go, and if you have the cash or finances to make up the difference since it would not have been included as part of your original financing.

However, we strongly advise that you do not bypass the design specification process unless you are considering a Cost Plus build model [see Ch. 14] for your project. This important process is what will truly allow you to compare apples to apples and ensure your price includes all of the creature comforts you desire.

3. Allowances

Allowances may be used during the pricing process, when selections are not made, prior to the commencement of contract or construction. First, let's be sure we understand what the term 'allowance' means, when used in the estimation process. First, we define allowance as "an amount specified and included in the construction contract for a certain item of work (e.g., appliances, lighting, flooring, etc.) whose details are not yet determined at the time of contracting."

If you have gone through a complete design specification process, you will inherently reduce the number of "allowances" in your overall scope of work; which we believe results in a better experience for both the builder and homeowner.

Because the specifications process requires significant time and resources, some builders may bypass the specifications process, and simply provide allowances for the estimate. Other times, a homeowner may not feel it's necessary to pay the architect, designer or builder, the design fee that is customary, to complete detailed specifications.

This is an area where we believe the buyer should beware! Allowances, when used as the **primary** budgeting process, often leave a lot more questions than answers and interpretation versus selection. Allowances also make it challenging to ensure that you are comparing apples to apples. So again, we recommend getting detailed specifications, versus using overly general allowances to budget a home building project.

When a builder provides a price that uses a lot of 'allowances' or has vague specifications, there is room for error, but quite often there is also a misunderstanding of the quality of products provided and/or change orders made. So, it is well worth the investment of time, money and resources to create detailed specifications. As you saw in Chapter 15, two houses with roughly the same square footage can vary <u>significantly</u> in the cost and quality of the home built.

With that said, it should be noted that, in some areas of the project, it may be standard practice to use *some* allowances, based on the overall design, quality, and scope of work. We believe it is important to have a clear understanding of any allowances used in your overall pricing to ensure that the allowances are <u>consistent</u> with your overall design preferences and specifications.

Now, when a quality, reputable builder meets with a client to discuss their expectations and offer an estimate, allowances may be required in some areas. However, it is important to understand that a **realistic** allowance is one that truly and consistently reflects the entire scope and quality of the job. For example, a customer who wants high-end finishes, custom millwork and top-quality materials is probably not going to want to use mid-grade appliances or fixtures in their kitchen or bath. So, the entire estimate and associated allowances are based on this consistency of quality. A $2M home will likely have Thermador or Wolf/Sub-Zero appliances versus GE or Kitchen-Aid. Too often, we see less reputable builders or contractors **under-estimating or using allowances for inferior products**. This can result in tens of thousands of dollars difference between one estimating proposal and another. You may not realize this at contract signing, but you will when those products are being ordered, delivered, and installed in your home. And, by that time, it's too late!

A quality, reputable builder understands that it's not just about winning the bid, it's about providing you a quality home building experience. They will work hard to ensure that your expectations are met every step of the way and with every product selection. So, again, if your estimates have more than 5-8% variance, we suggest you dig deeper or avoid this process altogether by investing in a complete set of design specifications.

Below is an example of what we have seen first-hand. In this case, the client's design and scope of work indicated a high-quality finish but there was a big difference between the pricing and allowances provided by Builder A vs. Builder B.

Here is what the client **saw** on the estimate and proposal (the gray areas of Quality were not shown on the proposals, but determined after the fact):

ALLOWANCES:					
Note: The *gray column of Quality* were not shown on the proposals, and only determined after the fact:					
Builder A			**Builder B**		
Product	Quality	**Price**	**Product**	Quality	**Price**
Cabinetry Double island, cabinets to ceiling, moldings, trim, glazing, finishes, custom design and fit options	A	$75,000	Cabinetry (Stock)	B	$60,000
Appliances (Sub-zero)	A	$45,000	Appliances (KitchenAid)	C	$20,000
Hardwood Flooring (Random width, character grade white oak)	A	$12.00/sf	Flooring (4" select red oak)	C	$8.00/sf
Windows	Clad	$60,000	Windows	Vinyl	$25,000
Heating/AC	A	$38,000	Heating/AC	A	$37,000

ALLOWANCES:						
Note: The *gray column of Quality* were not shown on the proposals, and only determined after the fact:						
Builder A			Builder B			
Product	Quality	**Price**	**Product**	Quality	**Price**	
Lighting (larger selection)	A	$15,000	Lighting	B	$12,000	
Plumbing Fixtures (larger selection)	A	$20,000	Plumbing Fixtures	B	$18,000	
Landscape/ Outdoor	A	$25,000	Landscape/ Outdoor	Omitted	$0	
		$278,000			$172,000	

There is a big difference in price and quality between the allowances provided by *Builder A* and Builder B but again, the client was not aware of the quality discrepancies. Now, it should be noted, that there is nothing wrong with 'choosing' a lower quality product, but allowances do not always clearly outline quality. (Again, that is the beauty of going through a complete design specification process before comparing builders.) However, in this case, the client was unaware of the quality each builder was quoting.

Instead, the client selected their builder solely based on price, which ultimately provided them a home with lower quality products, which is exactly what they paid for. This too, can have a major impact on the overall experience. Note that Builder A conscientiously includes higher quality products throughout the project bid while Builder B lowers the quality of certain products, in order to win the bid. This is an apples to oranges comparison and it happens every day in the industry, without detailed design specifications.

Now, in this case, the homeowner didn't seem to notice the quality until the lighting fixtures, plumbing fixtures and actual selections were being made. While making their final selections, they noticed that many of the options they wanted were only available as an upgrade. Since they were not included in the builder's original bid, they would have to upgrade many of their selections to the higher priced products. These upgrades were provided, but the cost was to be covered by cash out of pocket. This resulted in a number of change orders and a change order fee by the contractor. **At the end of the day, Builder B's project cost just as much, if not more, than if the homeowner had gone with Builder A.** This is a scenario we have seen happen to clients far too often and again reiterates the importance of creating consistent detailed specifications.

Authors Comments:
The *Estimating, Specifications and Allowances (ESA) process* is the most critical and complex area of the home building process, for client expectations, satisfaction, and ultimate home building experience. This is the single area where we have watched homeowners go for a lower price, without realizing what they were compromising. Investing in comprehensive design specifications will save you tremendous headaches and heartache.

Part 3

THE DESIGN PROCESS

Chapter 18:

An Overview of The Design Process

The design process is the foundation upon which your entire custom home building experience is built. As discussed previously, we believe it is important to start with a detailed list of design specifications. These detailed specifications help you:

- Ensure an apples to apples comparison for pricing

- Select the quality of the products you want to be used in your home

- Establish a budget and benchmarks for the final selections process

We believe the best custom home building experiences incorporate a design process that looks something like this:

1. Evaluate your overall budget and financing needs

2. Evaluate your lot requirements

3. Research and interview builders and architects you'd like to work with, narrowing it down to 1-3 choices

4. Contract either an architect or a builder to complete detailed design drawings and specifications

5. Compare builders, preliminary pricing, and choose the builder you'd like to begin a long-term relationship with

6. Refine your designs, with architect and builder collaboration, to finalize your budget

7. Consider whether a landscape architect and/or interior designer is needed for the project

8. Contract with your builder and begin your home building journey

Let's explore the design phase in further detail.

Chapter 19:

Builder & Architect Collaboration

col·lab·o·ra·tion (noun)
1. the action of working with someone to produce or create something.

We sincerely believe that genuine collaboration between an architect, a builder, and a homeowner can create a work of art! Isn't that, ultimately, what you want your home to be?

Over the past 30 years, we have utilized a variety of different business models. During this time, we have found that the collaborative approach provides varied and necessary input, experience, and ideas from both the builder and architect. It is through this collaboration that we build a well-designed home that is quality crafted and meets the homeowner's lifestyle and desired budget.

Some homeowners select an architect before they meet with a builder, while others select the builder and then have the builder assist them in selecting an architect. There is no inherently right or wrong way to proceed, but we ***strongly recommend*** that the builder and architect be *introduced early on* and *collaborate throughout the design process.* The architect is generally responsible for the design and structural elements of the home while the builder is primarily responsible for ensuring that the concept can be built within the budget desired. We believe this kind of collaboration is the key to a successful building experience and keeping the project within your budget and on-schedule.

Avoid making the mistake of contracting a builder or architect without interviewing **both** to ensure that they are willing, able, and eager to work together on your home. I remember a client who brought architectural drawings to us, ready and eager to begin construction. Unfortunately, we had to advise them that the home could not be built for the budget they had in mind. We suggested value-engineering aspects of the project to bring the design in line with their budget. The architect, in this situation, was adversarial and suggested they interview three more builders (who coincidentally also advised them that the designs and budget were not aligned.) This process wasted the homeowners time, money, and resources. As the project moved forward, this created an adversarial versus collaborative relationship which made the entire building process much more stressful for everyone involved. This situation could have been completely avoided if the architect and builder had been involved collaboratively early in the design process.

When interviewing your **builder**, ask them about the homes that they have worked collaboratively on, with an architect. Then, ask to speak with that architect about the builder's processes, craftsmanship, and accommodations for design. Ask your builder which architects they would recommend for your project. Likewise, when interviewing an **architect**, be sure to ask them about builders with whom they have worked collaboratively. Then, ask the builder if the architect's design concepts were efficient and realistic for the client's budgets and design concepts.

Be sure that your builder and architect are committed to a collaborative working relationship because this will have a great impact on your overall custom home building experience.

Authors Comments:
Some of the best projects are not a result of any earth-shattering construction material or technique, but rather a true collaboration between the architect, builder, and home-owner.

Chapter 20:

Prioritizing Needs vs. Wants

When you begin the design and budgeting process, it's important that you and your family have a clear understanding and priority of each other's needs vs. wants. We suggest using the *Design Preferences Checklist (Appendix Checklist #5)*. This should take about 30-60 minutes, but will save you a lot of time, arguments, and dollars! Using a spreadsheet is also ideal so you can rank and sort accordingly.

Each decision-maker should compile three lists - your needs, wants, dreams. Rank and prioritize the needs and wants accordingly. The dreams you will negotiate later, depending upon your budget requirements. After you have independently created your own list, get together and share your lists. There may be some things in common and there may be some things that are uniquely your own. You may need to compromise, based on your budget. The goal is to take time to review and discuss which items can be moved farther up or down the list to create one master list. This is the list you will ultimately review with your architect and builder.

As you begin to refine your design, incorporating your needs vs. wants, you will see where either your budget needs to be expanded, or your list of needs/wants needs to be reduced, depending upon your circumstances.

Your *Design Preferences Checklist* will help ensure your master design list incorporates all of the elements you've agreed on, as well as the few items that remain on your wants or dream list. This will make the entire design and budgeting process much easier for everyone involved.

Chapter 21:

Design Ideas & Considerations

When you think about designing your dream home and all of the unique features and elements you want to include, the fun part of building begins! What design elements do you want to incorporate into your dream home? The internet, social media, magazines and idea books can provide a wealth of ideas to consider, but it can also be a little overwhelming.

1. Design Selections

In the past, we would suggest that clients create a folder and throw in all the ideas, pictures and photos they wanted to discuss as part of the design. Today, it's much easier to pin, tag, and save these ideas to your phone, laptop or Pinterest board. Websites like Houzz and Wayfair are great places to start too! Since technology is always changing, and we want this book to be a relevant resource for years to come, we won't dive too deeply into specific applications, programs, or websites, but here are a few ways to simplify and organize the ideas you're considering.

Start an electronic file where you can keep all of your ideas and preferences. Separate ideas and photos into categories that correlate to the design selection process:

- Cabinets / Countertops
- Appliances
- Plumbing fixtures
- Exterior (Roof, Siding, Brick, Stone, Windows)
- Exterior Doors
- Stairs
- Fireplace
- Tile

- Interior Doors
- Baseboards, casings, other details
- Paint and stain
- Light fixtures
- Floor coverings
- Hardware (door and cabinet)

We've included a *Checklist for Design Preferences* (*Appendix Checklist #5*) that will help you define your design preferences and must-haves for each area. Review these design ideas and concepts with your architect and builder to allow them to get a sense of your style and also help ensure your tastes are aligned with your budget. We also find that introducing an interior designer, during the design phase, can be a tremendous asset to you.

2. Saving Pennies Without Watching the Dollars

Another common misperception is when the homeowner's focus on saving pennies without watching the dollars. Consider this example:

Many years ago, Terry and Bill met with us to review their plans and sign the construction contract. Terry had lots of questions about the costs of the selections included in our estimate. She felt that she could buy products online at a fraction of the cost, thereby saving significant money. We explained that while there may be some savings, there would be inherent problems with this approach. In addition to the fact that we could not warranty those products, they would need to ensure the selections arrived in accordance with the construction schedule. She insisted that she wanted to go this route and, hesitantly, we agreed, despite our disclosed concerns.

As the project progressed, Terry found the selection process to be very challenging. She struggled with almost every decision and was unable to make selections in a timely manner in accordance with the construction schedule. We suggested that perhaps a designer could assist her in expediting the process, but she wanted to 'save money' and choose her own products on line.

As an example of the logistic concerns, when we were ready to install fixtures in the bathrooms, the products Terry chose were back-ordered, delayed, or in some cases, not in working order. Because the plumbing fixtures were not onsite, and couldn't be installed, the tile work was delayed and the plumber had to make multiple visits to the job site, costing additional time and money. Since the tile work was delayed, the glass and flooring couldn't be installed and so on.

This process pushed the entire schedule back 8 weeks– which required them to extend their construction loan, which ultimately cost them far more than whatever savings she had anticipated.

Needless to say, this experience taught us a few valuable lessons. First, specification selections must be made upfront and in accordance with an agreed-upon timeline. Second, we provide all the materials, so that we can work with our suppliers to ensure timely delivery and quality assurance. Third, after this experience, we implemented our complimentary Client Concierge process to help our clients with the selection process, which greatly enhances the customer experience.

3. Design Considerations

The design of your home is a significant representation of you and your family, your status, and more importantly your lifestyle. So, there are a number of design considerations that should be made with the goal of providing a home that will enhance your lifestyle and also provide the most value for your budget or investment. In our experience, the following design considerations will help you allocate your square footage, priorities, and budgets accordingly:

1. **Design Services** – A qualified interior designer can help you maximize and allocate your budget, find unique one-of-a-kind items, and help you make selections that will allow your home to be uniquely yours. Why spend $2M on a home and not enlist the services of a designer to help you customize it to your liking?

2. **Kitchen** – this is the focal point of the home. Whether you like to cook or not, the kitchen is the gathering place and center of activity for homework, holidays, and entertaining. I have never had a client say their kitchen was too big, had too much storage, or too many features. In addition, your kitchen can also provide the biggest return on investment, for resale value. Avoid skimping on the budget for your kitchen. Choosing high-quality cabinets, appliances, and countertops are always a good investment. Add unique design elements in the millwork, lighting, and special features! Make it uniquely yours and create a spacious environment where everyone will want to be!

3. **Family Room** – this is the area of your home that will accommodate family and guests every day, at all times of the year. Be sure to oversize and leave plenty of room for furnishings and cozy lounging. If you have to sacrifice room or square footage, don't do it here! Make concessions in other areas of the home,

but leave the kitchen and family room big enough to accommodate your largest gathering. You'll be glad you did!

4. **Bath Rooms** – the more the merrier when it comes to bathrooms, as everyone in the house likes to have privacy and creature comforts. Even if you have to make concessions on the *size* of the bathrooms to have more of them, it can often pay off in the long run.

5. **Bedrooms** – Be sure your rooms are designed to accommodate the furniture you have or desire leaving plenty of space for the bed, dressers, armoire, etc. However, bedrooms don't need to be overly large, as a smaller amount of our time is actually spent here – instead, use the additional space for...

6. **Roomy Closets** – Spacious walk-in closets, dressing rooms, and designer-inspired display shelving make an ordinary closet extraordinary.

7. **Fixtures** – Quality lighting, hardware, and plumbing fixtures often provide the perfect accent to a room's overall design.

8. **Storage** – Most homeowners accumulate 'stuff' and when building a new home, they often underestimate the amount of storage they need. Be sure to consider your current and future storage requirements and discuss these with your architect/builder. It costs very little to add in unfinished areas for storage.

Chapter 22:

Final Selections

During the first part of the design phase, when you created your design specifications, you made selections about which quality of product to use in your home. Although you chose the specifications, such as whether you want to use granite or quartz for your countertops, you now get to truly 'customize' your home, by making the final selections – choosing the actual colors and materials that will be used to make your home a one-of-a-kind work of art, designed just for you.

This part of the process can be exciting! However, for some clients, it is may also be challenging. After all, in the average 5,000 square foot custom home, there may be 30 different categories of selections that need to be made and another 30-50 choices within each category. Your *Checklist for Design Preferences (Appendix Checklist #5)* can help organize your thoughts to start you thinking about this process and, as we've suggested previously, a digital file that keeps all of your pictures and ideas can be a great resource during the selection process.

1. Client Concierge

In our firm, we also provide a Client Concierge to assist with this process. The Client Concierge helps enhance the communication flowing between the builder, project manager, client, and trusted vendors. The Client Concierge also sets appointments for you, at the showrooms where we have established relationships. The Client Concierge may also assist you throughout the selections process.

If you elect to work with an interior designer, they can be invaluable during the final selection process, discussing the pros/

cons of each selection and providing guidance on color schemes, how to incorporate existing furniture, and making recommendations about ideal products for your family's lifestyle.

2. Making Selections & Keeping the Schedule On-Track

The selection process is a critical component of keeping your construction on-schedule. While this process is not set in stone, we have found that it works best when followed as closely as possible. It will keep you on track on focused on the tasks at hand and keep your construction project on schedule. We typically break the selection process down into the following phases such as:

- Cabinets / Countertops
- Appliances
- Plumbing fixtures
- Exterior (Roof, Siding, Brick, Stone, Windows)
- Exterior Doors
- Stairs
- Fireplace
- Tile
- Interior Doors
- Baseboards, casings, other details
- Paint and stain
- Light fixtures
- Floor coverings
- Hardware (door and cabinet)

Authors Comments:
We believe that a client concierge, if provided by your builder, can take away a lot of the stress often caused by this part of the process. We also have found that clients who work with an interior designer, often have a much better overall experience. Streamlining the selection process, and making your selections in a timely manner, is a critical element to keep your project on schedule.

Chapter 23:

Should You Consider An Interior Designer?

When you consider the countless hours, resources, and money that are invested in the entire luxury custom home experience, it just doesn't make a lot of sense to cut corners on the interior design. Many homeowners are under the misconception that interior design should come <u>after</u> the home is built. Nothing could be further from the truth!

Let's use a quick analogy – let's say you are in the market to buy a luxury boat. You determine the brand, size, overall length, and mechanical specifications. Do you wait until the boat is completely manufactured and delivered to determine the color of the hull, seats, carpet, cabinetry or countertops? No! Of course not, all of that is discussed during the design phase before the boat is ordered. So, why would you reverse the process when buying an even larger luxury item, like a custom home?

It makes a lot of sense to include the interior designer as part of the overall design process so that proper thought can be given to design elements, furnishings, room sizes, and other details, while the overall design is being considered. An interior designer can often provide valuable input and enhance your overall vision and goals. They are also adept at considering your current furnishings and design elements and integrating them with the new space. A well-informed and experienced designer will typically help you with material and finish selections, lighting, flooring, and more!

I remember a client that came to us, a few years ago, with architectural drawings in hand, and ready to build a 6,000 square foot home. The project went smoothly, was finished on-time, and the keys were handed over. A short time later, the client called to ask if we could enlarge the master bedroom. I was surprised and asked them what they were looking to accomplish? She explained that they had some family heirloom furniture that was overcrowding the space and either they would have to get rid of some of the furniture or enlarge the space. An interior designer would almost certainly have vetted this requirement out early in the design process.

Another client moved into their new home and realized that there were no feature walls suited to showcase some of their extensive artwork collection. Both of these stories demonstrate the value of working with an interior designer, as part of the design process.

Just like the architect and builder, the designer must work collaboratively with the goal of providing the homeowner with the best experience and the most beautifully crafted home possible. Your interior designer can serve as a valuable resource and guide to take a beautifully built space and transform it into a home that is uniquely yours. The interior designer can add the finishing touches that bring the custom home building experience full-circle to enhance your home and lifestyle.

Ask your builder or architect for recommendations on interior designers they have worked within the past. You won't regret it!

Part 4

THE CONSTRUCTION PROCESS

Chapter 24:

Overview of the Construction Process

We have discussed many concepts so far, in this book, but below we provide an "Executive Summary" recap of the overall construction process:

- **Phase 1 – Financing**

  Before you begin designing a home, you've got to know how much home you can afford. If you have unlimited financial resources, you can skip this step, but if not, make sure you consider your financial situation before you begin anything. Don't look for or buy land, meet with an architect, or start interviewing builders until you've determined your overall budget. There is no point designing a $5 Million home if you can only afford a $2 Million home. We have devoted Part 2 of this book to Budgeting and Financing, so be sure to read that material and meet with your lender before you begin the process. This will save you time and money, in the long run, and help you plan accordingly.

- **Phase 2 – Selecting Your Builder**

  As we discussed in Part 1, the selection of your builder is an important long-term relationship. You'll want to be sure your builder is competent, reputable, uses a solid construction process, and knows how to run their business. More importantly, they should be involved during the design process for the most collaboration.

- **Phase 3 – Design**

  Many homeowners are eager to get their designs on paper and see their dreams come to life. Some homeowners select an architect before they meet with a builder, while others select a builder they want to work with, and then have the builder assist them in selecting an architect. We recommend that the builder and architect be *introduced early on* and *collaborate throughout the design process*. The architect is generally responsible for the design and structural elements of the home while the builder is primarily responsible for ensuring that the concept can be built within the budget desired. We believe this kind of collaboration is the key to a successful building experience. We highly recommend having either the builder or architect complete detailed designed specifications before the project begins.

- **Phase 4 – Pricing**

  We discuss pricing in detail in Part 2 and specifically explore hidden costs, vague specifications, and more. At the end of the day, one builder's pricing should not be more than 5-8% from another's, if all things are equal. If you find a builder that says they can build a home for dramatically less than another – beware!

- **Phase 5 – Permitting**

  Each jurisdiction has specific criteria that must be met for the permitting process. Some areas have more fees, some areas have more restrictions, and some areas must comply with critical area or forest regulations. Your builder should be well versed in these requirements and be able to give you information and estimates for the home and Lot.

- **Phase 6 – Construction Process Begins**

  If you've done your homework and selected a reputable and experienced builder, the construction process should be smooth sailing but it certainly helps if your expectations are also managed along the way.

- **Phase 7 – End of Construction**

5 Keys to Success

Now that you understand the phases of the custom home building process, here are what we believe to be the five keys to success:

1. Educating yourself so that you understand the overall process and have reasonable expectations.

2. Selecting a quality and reputable builder (in accordance with Part 1 of this book) with experience, processes, and utilization of best practices to deliver your dream home.

3. The collaboration of the architect and builder at the earliest stage possible, preferably during the design phase.

4. Working with the architect or builder to provide a *detailed list of design specifications*. This will be integral to the overall pricing, experience, and final selection processes.

5. Making selections and decisions quickly to keep the project running smoothly and on-time.

Chapter 25:

Construction Schedule

In a perfect world, your house would be built in a timely fashion with no weather delays, no hiccups, or complications. But, in the real world, there are always moving pieces that must be dealt with, during the construction process, that will impact the timeline, resources, and/or budget. This is another area where having a well-qualified, experienced builder who can adapt and prepare for these changes along the way will help reduce your stress and add to your overall experience. There is just nothing more comforting than knowing that you are in capable hands. But, there are some things you can do to help the process along.

Although every project is unique, when building a custom home, your builder will produce a complete construction schedule. There are some basic phases included in every project that must be accomplished in an orderly fashion. These phases include:

1. Design, Site Planning & Budgeting
2. Permitting
3. Footings, Foundation & Framing
4. Mechanical, Plumbing & Electric Systems/Rough-Ins
5. Insulation & Drywall
6. Interior Doors, Trim & Millwork
7. Painting
8. Tilework & Flooring
9. Electric & Smart Home Systems
10. Flooring & Millwork
11. Paint, Fixtures & Appliances
12. Completion

We typically create a construction schedule that provides a

timeline for each of these phases so that you will have a rough idea of what is going to happen and when. It is worth noting that, as discussed previously, the final selections must be made in a timely manner, in order to keep the schedule on track.

Your personalized construction schedule will be created after your construction agreement is signed. At that time, you will also receive a final selections schedule so that you can do your part to keep the project running smoothly.

Any questions you have should be discussed at the beginning of this process with the understanding that the schedule is fluid, based on weather conditions, selections made, and other factors that may impact the overall schedule.

Chapter 26:

How Long Will the Construction Process Take?

There is no simple answer to this question as each home has different criteria that will impact the construction schedule. So, the best answer to this question is the answer that your trusted builder provides, with the understanding that the schedule is fluid and will be adjusted based on a variety of conditions and factors. The construction schedule provided by your builder will give you a rough idea about the timelines.

Some counties have an extensive permitting process that takes additional time that must be added to the construction schedule. Site work is contingent on site conditions and soil testing and can add weeks to the schedule.

Waterfront homes, in particular, can take much longer to construct, since the builder must comply with specifications, inspections, and guidelines specifically for critical areas on the Bay. Forest preservation or conservation areas require special variances or permitting.

Weather is another factor that can significantly impact the construction schedule so it's important to manage your own expectations and timelines with this in mind.

One of the most critical ways homeowners can have a positive or negative impact on the construction schedule is by making their final selections in a timely manner.

Chapter 27:

Avoiding Common Mistakes During Construction

1. **Select a Great Builder** – We just can't reiterate enough how important the builder is to the overall construction experience. If you've done a thorough job of selecting a great builder that will quarterback your construction project through common challenges, they will also have the knowledge, experience, and resources, to make appropriate adjustments as needed.

2. **Avoid Second Guessing Your Builder** – When it comes to the products, materials, sub-contractors, vendors or resources your builder uses, you've got to be able to trust and leave them alone to do their work! Your builder is responsible for the construction process. The builder has established business relationships that can be relied upon to deliver on-time and warranty their products. Don't try to micro-manage the project and second guess every resource. You will end up costing yourself and your builder time and money.

3. **Make Decisions & Selections In A Timely Manner** – During construction, there will be a number of decisions and selections you'll need to make. Make these decisions by the agreed-upon deadlines. If you're planning a vacation, get it done before you leave. Many homeowners struggle with selections, so as mentioned earlier, we highly recommend enlisting the services of an interior designer to assist you. But, whatever you do, don't delay or postpone

these decisions as the construction schedule will be negatively impacted.

4. **Communicate with Your Builder** – Communication is a key part of the building process. If you have a question or concern, don't let it fester. Discuss it with your builder and/or project manager right away. However, it's important to give your builder or project manager the autonomy to carry out their work without constant interruption.

5. **Avoid Providing Direction to Sub-Contractors** – You will likely be provided a primary point of contact for the duration of your construction, either the builder or an on-site superintendent. This person will have detailed knowledge of every aspect of your project. Avoid giving orders or providing direction to sub-contractors – they are simply doing what they have been instructed to do, and have no frame of reference for the overall project. Your direction could delay the job, cause confusion, and sometimes even cost you more money!

6. **Avoid Using Customer's Own Sub-Contractors or Materials** – Most builders do not allow for substitution of customer's own materials, because ultimately the builder is responsible for keeping the project on-time and on-budget. When a customer tries to supply their own materials or sub-contractors, there are inherent problems, not the least of which, is the fact that the builder cannot warranty these products and services. If you are expecting a high quality, well-constructed home, let your builder provide you the products, services, and tradesmen they rely upon time after time.

7. **Change Order Process** – During construction, if you request changes from the original design and scope of the project, a change order will be required to enact those changes. Understand your builder's change order process, and the impact your change order may have on the overall production schedule. We discuss this in further detail in Chapter 27.

8. **Managing Hours of the Workers** - Don't expect workers to be on-site every day from 7:00 am to 4:00 pm. Again, the construction schedule is a fluid element and a delay in one area may impact or delay other areas. If inspections are occurring or the weather has impacted the schedule, workers may have to push or rearrange their schedules accordingly. It is the goal of your builder to move the project along as quickly *and effectively* as possible. Consult your builder with questions, but avoid trying to micro-manage the construction schedule.

Chapter 28:

Change Orders

The inherent nature of the custom home building process is to accommodate change orders as the home's construction project progresses. The experienced custom home builder will be able to accommodate these requests and adapt the schedule as needed.

It is important to note that, for most reputable builders, change orders are performed *as a service to the client*. They are not a profit-making component. Quite the opposite is true. The widely held perception, in the industry, is that change orders are an area of high profit to builders. This may be the case for some, but not for most builders. The margin added to a change order rarely recoups the associated time and administrative resources required to accommodate the change order. As a matter of fact, most builders would prefer to build a home without any change orders, but the nature of the custom home building process is to provide the homeowner with the ability to customize the home to their desired liking, even during construction.

Change orders can alter the construction schedule, push production timelines, and may cause a ripple effect in many other areas of the project so it's imperative to consider each change order's cost and impact on the overall construction schedule.

For example, one client decided, after the house was under roof, and they were able to walk the space, that they really wanted additional square footage on the main level. Although we were willing and able to accommodate this change, it required a big shift to the existing schedule - a set-back to the overall schedule by about 6-8 weeks. Why? Additional site work had to be done, another foundation had to be poured, and the framers and roofers would have to be re-engaged to come back out to build the additional space. Construction on the rest of the home would be brought to a stand-still until all of these changes were made, so that construction and inspections could be re-synchronized. Accommodating this change required good communication, flexibility on the part of the builder and client, and precise execution of this change order to be effective. Now, this is obviously a dramatic example of a change order and how it impacts the overall construction. However, it's important for the client to understand that even the smallest changes can have a ripple effect on the construction process and delivery time-frames. Multiple change orders can side-track an otherwise smooth project, so it's important for the builder and the client to discuss change orders, as they arise, and to make these decisions with discernment and flexibility for its impact on the overall process.

It's also worth noting that most change orders are not included as part of the original financing of the home. So, in many cases, change orders will require either the homeowner to pay these costs out of pocket or to communicate with their lender about ways to cover these costs in the financing.

Almost every custom home project will have some element of change orders because many custom homeowners evolve their decisions as the project progresses. In many cases, these changes enhance the project as the homeowner begins to touch and feel this evolution. But, the wise homeowner will carefully consider any change order decisions and their overall impact on the construction process and discuss these changes with the builder to help manage their overall expectations.

Chapter 29:

End of Construction

As your home nears completion, the emotions are at an all-time high! You are likely to experience excitement and anticipation about moving into your home while having to deal with the stress or anxiety of coordinating the physical move itself, setting up services like electric, cable, etc. and perhaps even selling your existing home. This range of emotions can cause an otherwise pleasant experience to become highly stressful. Our first advice is to take a deep breath!

While your home may be scheduled for 'turn-over' on the 1st of the month, there are still major construction issues occurring that are fluid, so the timeline must continue to remain flexible. No builder wants to turn over a home that hasn't been properly punched out, quality checked, and completed – nor does a homeowner want to receive such a home. So, here are our best suggestions for the end of the construction process.

1. **Lock Out** – Many builders will respectfully 'lockout' the client during the final month of construction, similar to an HGTV style reveal. This is an important step for you and your builder. Finishing touches are being made to all of the elements of your home. The final coat of paint, the final finish on the flooring, quality checks on the mechanical systems, and the meticulous attention to details are all underway. This is not the time to have you, the kids, the dogs, or the in-laws running through the home and unintentionally causing delays.

   We had a client enter a home that was near turn-over (the process of turning the home over to the client).

The floors had just been finished and the final touch-ups were being completed. The site was still muddy, sod had not been laid, and the family's dog got in the home, by accident. Needless to say, the flooring contractors had to be rescheduled to come out to clean and rebuff the floors. The turn-over was pushed back by two weeks.

On another project, the homeowner entered the home before the quality control checks were complete, and was emotionally distraught that some of the lights weren't working and a faucet was leaking. Their anxiety was unnecessary because these items were still being addressed, as part of the quality control process. We have found the lock-out process helps the builder bring the project to a successful conclusion, reduce unnecessary stress, and potential delays. It also provides an overall better experience, in the long run, when your home is 'revealed' to you, in it's completed condition, as intended.

2. **Quality Control** - Let the builder do their job for completion including final quality checks, final inspections, punchout. Don't rush this process. Just as your home took 8-12 months or longer to execute the construction, the quality control process is an important final step in the construction process. This phase should not be rushed because you need to move in.

3. **Reconciling Budget and Change Orders** – Before the home is turned over, the entire budget must be reconciled and payment for all change orders agreed upon. Anticipate this phase so that you are prepared financially for this reconciliation process.

4. **Organized Chaos** – Even prior to lock-out, there is routine mayhem going on towards the conclusion of the project. Smart homeowners will recognize that this is a normal part of the completion process towards the end of construction and reserve emotions for the final reveal.

5. **Safety** – As the project nears completion, there may be safety issues as the mechanical and electrical systems are checked, stair railings are secured, and final inspections are occurring. Adhere to your builder's requests regarding entering the property at any time during this final phase.

Chapter 30:

The Final Reveal

The final reveal is scheduled and you are ready to take occupancy of the home you've always dreamed of! This is the day you've waited for! This home will be a true reflection of your lifestyle and the keys to your own unique, one-of-a-kind, custom home will be handed over to you to enjoy for years to come. This is truly the culmination of the entire experience!

As you stroll through your new home, you will likely recall every detail, every decision, every choice along the way for many years to come! Your builder will guide you through the home and the inner workings of each room. You will review the mechanical, electrical and plumbing systems, and ask questions along the way.

This process typically takes several hours, so we advise leaving the dogs and kids at home, or having them join you after the turn-over process is complete. There will be a lot of information to digest and you should also receive a binder, during the turn-over process, with manuals for appliances, warranty information, etc. This is also a great time to understand the process for any service requests as you get settled into your new home.

In true HGTV fashion, your final reveal will be a swarm of emotions for all that you've accomplished. Be sure to take photos and capture these moments! And, most importantly...

Enjoy your new home!

Conclusion

Well, now that you've read the book, do you feel like you are better-equipped to explore the custom home building process? Do you understand the value of collaboration between the architect and builder? Do you have a better understanding of the complex process, the importance of logistics, and some of the ways in which you can contribute to a positive experience? If so, then we have accomplished our goal!

Paul Mueller, Jr.
President,
Mueller Homes

We have worked hard to distill the information we've learned over the past few decades in a concise, easy-to-read format. We've tried to provide the good, the bad, and even the ugly because goodness knows, we've seen it all! And, as my father said in the introduction, one of our biggest goals in writing this book is to help you, the reader, avoid the painful and sometimes, tragic horror stories that plague too many homeowners and sometimes, inexperienced builders.

Building a custom luxury home is, for many people, a once-in-a-lifetime experience and a significant investment. It is a very personal, thoughtful, and exciting process that truly reflects your lifestyle, success, and achievement. We hope that we've been able to educate you as well as inspire you. Most of all, we hope we have shown you...

How to Create an Experience You'll Love to Remember!

Part 5

CHECKLISTS

All checklists can be downloaded at MuellerHomes.com

Checklist # 1:

QUESTIONS TO ASK A POTENTIAL BUILDER

Download this checklist at www.MuellerHomes.com

☐	How many years in construction?
☐	How many custom homes have you built?
☐	What is average price of homes you build? Highest? _____ Lowest?_____
☐	How many years running this business?
☐	Describe your design process?
☐	What is your construction process like?
☐	Which architects have you worked with?
☐	How will you help me keep my project on budget?
☐	What is the biggest challenge you've seen customers face?
☐	List of references for similar homes in past 3 years?
☐	Can I tour one of your previously built homes?

Checklist #1:

QUESTIONS TO ASK A POTENTIAL BUILDER (continued)

☐	Describe the "money" process for building a home. How do you segregate funds by customer or project?
☐	How do you keep the project on-schedule?
☐	What makes you different or unique from other builders in the area?
☐	Tell me about the best/worst projects you've ever done? Why?
☐	Who is responsible for oversight and day-to-day management of the project?
☐	Describe your warranty policy.
☐	Do you offer a client concierge?
☐	Have you ever worked with a landscape architect?
☐	Have you ever worked with an interior designer?

Checklist # 2:

QUESTIONS TO ASK BUILDER'S REFERENCES

Download this checklist at www.MuellerHomes.com

☐	What is your overall rating (1-5) of this builder?
☐	What was the best part about working with this builder?
☐	If you had it to do over again, what would you change?
☐	How well did your builder: • Stay on-schedule? • Communicate with you? • Demonstrate Honesty/Integrity • Commitment to Quality?
☐	What would you say were the driving factors behind your decision to choose THIS builder?
☐	How many builders did you interview before selecting this builder?
☐	How was the financial aspect of the process? Draws? Deposits?
☐	Have you had any service or warranty issues?
☐	How did the builder respond to problems?

Checklist # 2:

QUESTIONS TO ASK BUILDER'S <u>REFERENCES</u> (continued)

☐	What type of home did you build and how long ago was it? (Square footage, budget range, the complexity of design, etc. – make sure this is similar to the type of home you're looking to build)
☐	Here are some great ways to ask for feedback from client references: • Can you tell me about your experience with the builder? (Leave this question completely open-ended and let the client talk) • Did you have a good relationship with the builder? Was the builder trustworthy? • What were the best aspects of working with this builder? • What were some of the limitations you felt this builder had? • Did you ever regret choosing this builder? Why or why not?
☐	Would you build again with or recommend this builder?

Checklist # 3:

QUESTIONS TO ASK A POTENTIAL ARCHITECT

Download this checklist at www.MuellerHomes.com

	Question	What You Are Looking For...
☐	How many years in business?	You want an experienced architect.
☐	How many custom homes have you designed?	Have they designed the type of home you're looking to build?
☐	What is the average price or budget range of homes you design? Highest? _____ Lowest?_____	
☐	At what point do you typically get a builder involved in the process?	The collaboration between the architect and builder is key to a smooth process and experience.
☐	Are you involved during the construction process?	If you have a qualified builder and the architect has provided detailed specifications, this may or may not be necessary.
☐	What has been your experience working with builders?	Ensure a collaborative approach.
☐	Tell me about the budgeting process for design work.	Typically, the builder needs to be involved early on to ensure the design is within a certain budget.

Checklist # 3:

QUESTIONS TO ASK A POTENTIAL <u>ARCHITECT</u> (continued)

	Question	What You Are Looking For...
☐	How can you help me ensure that the home we design can be built within my budget?	Make sure the architect is designing a house you can afford and works collaboratively with your builder.
☐	What does the design process look like when you're taking our visions and putting them on paper?	
☐	How much do you charge to create detailed design specifications?	
☐	What is your fee structure for a project of this type?	

Checklist # 4:

QUESTIONS ABOUT <u>FINANCING</u>

Download this checklist at www.MuellerHomes.com

	Question	What You Are Looking For...
☐	How many years have you been doing construction financing?	You want someone very experienced in construction lending, not just regular loans
☐	Are there one or two settlements?	Two settlements generally have more associated costs, but are sometimes necessary depending on the project.
☐	What are the terms offered?	
☐	What are the down payment requirements?	
☐	What are terms for short-term, while home is being built?	
☐	Is the rate locked during construction or does it float?	
☐	What are the terms *after* the home is completed?	Do you have a locked rate for the permanent loan? How does this affect you in a rising or declining rate environment?
☐	Do you have a construction fee/ administrative fee?	
☐	What are the draw fees?	
☐	Describe the draw process?	

Checklist # 4:

QUESTIONS ABOUT <u>FINANCING</u> (continued)

	Question	What You Are Looking For...
☐	Are there any fees for converting the loan from a construction loan to a permanent mortgage?	
☐	Is there an option for a float-down if the rates improve?	
☐	Is the permanent rate locked at the beginning of construction?	
☐	What happens if my build takes longer than expected? Extension fees?	

Checklist #5:

DESIGN PREFERENCES

Download this checklist at www.MuellerHomes.com

Suggestion: It may be helpful to start a spreadsheet using these main areas, with two columns, denoting your **needs** vs. **wants**. The average couple will often start out with different priorities and lists, so it is sometimes advisable for each person to develop their own list and then work together to create one master list that is agreed upon ahead of time. This master list can then be used as the basis for discussions with your builder. Your builder will be able to help you value engineer any items on the list to facilitate your budget and suggest any other options for consideration.

☐	Floor Plans & Overall Design
☐	Architectural Details
☐	Will You Work With an Interior Designer?

Checklist #5:

DESIGN PREFERENCES (continued)

		Needs	Wants
☐	Exteriors		
	Roofing Windows Siding		
☐	Kitchen		
	Appliances Countertops Cabinetry Lighting Bar/Island/Eat-In Kitchen Flooring Butler Pantry Plumbing Fixtures Lighting Fixtures		
☐	Bathrooms		
	Cabinetry Sinks Showers/Tubs Tile Work Flooring Sauna/Steam Shower His/Hers Plumbing Fixtures Lighting Fixtures		

Checklist #5:

DESIGN PREFERENCES (continued)

		Needs	Wants
☐	Bedrooms		
	Number EnSuite Flooring Ceiling Height Size Closets		
☐	Living Spaces		
	Ceiling Height Flooring Fireplaces Acoustics Lifestyle Accommodations		
☐	Finishes		
	Paint or Wood Grade Millwork & Trim Details Colors Built-Ins		

Checklist #5:

DESIGN PREFERENCES (continued)

		Needs	Wants
☐	Flooring & Railings		
	Stairs to Match Finish Wood, Iron or Custom Railings Heated Designated Materials		
☐	Millwork & Trim Details		
	Custom Closets Built-Ins Gingerbread		
☐	Special Accommodations		
	Age-in-Place Wheelchair Accessible Special Needs		
☐	Outdoor Living		
	Pool Hardscapes Landscaping Driveway Decks/Porches Lighting or Sound		

Checklist #5:

DESIGN PREFERENCES (continued)

		Needs	Wants
☐	Garage		
	# of Bays Temperature Controlled Workshop Dog Wash Area		
☐	Other Amenities		
	Basement Gym or Workout Room Media/Entertainment Room Game Room or Kids Play Room Area Wine Cellar A/V or Security Sunroom Piano Room Detached Garage		
☐	Additional Considerations		

ABOUT MUELLER HOMES

Since 1992, Mueller Homes has been handcrafting distinctive custom homes and luxury estates throughout Maryland.

With a strong tradition founded upon distinctive craftsmanship and a finely-tuned construction process, Mueller Homes has exceeded the expectations of clients year after year and won numerous awards. As the business has grown over the years, so has the exclusive list of clientele served.

We take a lot of pride in our company's history and longevity but our reputation for delivering an extraordinary experience is what truly sets us apart! We understand that the client relationship is vital to that process. We work tirelessly to earn our client's trust and respect and to deliver a beautiful, quality home that is built with the most exceptional craftsmanship. That is truly what has allowed us to be successful.

As a family-owned business, Paul Mueller, Sr. was able to mentor and teach Paul Mueller, Jr. all of the important lessons as they worked side by side for many years. By instilling the same strong core values, work ethic, and client-centered vision, the tradition of excellence and client focus will continue for generations to come!

Our homes are an extension of our client's lifestyles. There is a tremendous amount of thought and emotion that go into every decision. That creates an opportunity to provide our clients with a very personalized experience and we take that responsibility seriously. It's so rewarding to be able to share that experience and know that we've provided them something they will cherish for years to come! That is what is truly unique about Mueller Homes.

Experience the Extraordinary! If you'd like to build your dream home, contact Mueller Homes today! Handcrafting Homes for Your Lifestyle.

Learn more about us at www.MuellerHomes.com

www.ingramcontent.com/pod-product-compliance
Lightning Source LLC
Chambersburg PA
CBHW021844090426
42811CB00033B/2138/J